BUILD WEB APPLICATION WITH DJANGO

A Beginner's Guide to Python-Powered Web Development

THOMPSON CARTER

TABLE OF CONTENTS

CHAPTER 9: DJANGO TEMPLATES AND RENDERING HTML

CHAPTER 11: WORKING WITH STATIC AND MEDIA FILES 130

CHAPTER 14: BUILDING REST APIS WITH DJANGO REST FRAMEWORK 176

CHAPTER 16: OPTIMIZING DJANGO PERFORMANCE 189

CHAPTER 19: INTEGRATING WEB SOCKETS FOR REAL-TIME FEATURES 222

INTRODUCTION: BUILDING WEB APPLICATIONS WITH DJANGO

Overview of Web Development Fundamentals

In the world of technology, web development is an essential skill that powers everything from personal blogs to sophisticated online platforms that serve millions of users daily. At its core, web development is about creating websites or applications that are accessible through a web browser. These sites and apps range from static websites, where content is fixed and unchanging, to dynamic web applications that allow user interaction, data manipulation, and real-time updates.

Understanding the Client-Server Model

Web development is built upon the client-server model, a fundamental structure that defines how data is communicated across the internet. In this model, a **client** is the end-user device (like a laptop or smartphone) that requests resources, while the **server** is the machine that hosts and provides these resources. When a user enters a website URL into their browser, they are sending a request to the server hosting that site. The server then processes this request, retrieves the relevant data, and sends it back to the client, where it is rendered in the browser.

This process is largely powered by **HTTP (Hypertext Transfer Protocol)**, a set of rules that allows web servers and clients to communicate. Each time a user clicks a link, submits a form, or loads a page, an HTTP request is sent from the client to the server. The server responds with the requested resources or, in some cases, with error messages if something goes wrong.

Differentiating Between Front-End and Back-End

Web development is often divided into **front-end** and **back-end** development. Front-end development focuses on the aspects of a web application that users interact with directly. This includes designing the layout, implementing user interfaces, and ensuring the website is responsive and visually appealing. Technologies like HTML, CSS, and JavaScript power the front-end, creating dynamic and interactive elements that enhance user experience.

In contrast, **back-end development** is concerned with the server-side logic, data storage, and processing that power the front-end. The back-end manages user requests, interacts with the database, and ensures data security and application functionality. Back-end development often involves working with databases (like MySQL or PostgreSQL), server languages (like Python, PHP, or Ruby), and frameworks (like Django or Flask) that streamline application development.

The Evolution of Web Development Frameworks

The web has come a long way from the static, text-heavy websites of the early 1990s. As websites evolved, developers began to demand more powerful tools to build dynamic applications that could handle complex interactions and process large amounts of data. This need for efficiency and reliability led to the creation of web frameworks.

A **web development framework** is a software tool that provides pre-built components and libraries, allowing developers to build applications quickly and efficiently. Frameworks handle common tasks like form validation, URL routing, database interactions, and security, freeing developers from repetitive coding and allowing them to focus on unique application features. Frameworks also encourage consistent coding practices, making development faster and the resulting applications more robust.

Popular frameworks include **Ruby on Rails**, **Laravel** (PHP), and **Django** (Python), each catering to a specific language and set of needs. These frameworks gained traction due to their ability to simplify complex tasks, offer ready-made solutions for common issues, and speed up development. Today, frameworks are indispensable tools in the web developer's toolkit.

What Django Is and Why It's Valuable

Django, a high-level Python web framework, is one of the most popular frameworks for building web applications today. Originally released in 2005, Django has been used by developers worldwide to create everything from small websites to massive platforms serving millions of users. Django's philosophy is simple: **make it easier to build web applications quickly and securely**. Its motto, "The web framework for perfectionists with deadlines," reflects this goal, aiming to provide tools that are both powerful and easy to use.

The Power of Django: Features and Benefits

One of Django's standout qualities is its **"batteries-included" philosophy**. This approach means that Django comes with a comprehensive set of tools and libraries, often eliminating the need to rely on third-party packages for common functionalities. Whether it's user authentication, form handling, or URL routing, Django includes robust, ready-to-use modules for each.

Django is also **secure by default**. Security is a major concern in web development, especially for applications handling sensitive user information. Django includes built-in protection against many common vulnerabilities, such as SQL injection, cross-site scripting (XSS), and cross-site request forgery (CSRF). This makes Django a preferred choice for developers prioritizing security.

Another critical strength of Django is its **scalability**. Django applications can start small and grow into complex, large-scale applications without needing a complete architectural overhaul. The framework's modularity, combined with Python's flexibility, allows developers to scale efficiently, making Django suitable for applications that handle high traffic and large volumes of data.

Django's MVT Architecture: The Model-View-Template Pattern

Django follows a specific software design pattern known as **Model-View-Template (MVT)**, which is slightly different from the more widely known **Model-View-Controller (MVC)** pattern. Understanding Django's MVT pattern is essential for grasping how it organizes data, user interfaces, and application logic.

- **Model**: The Model layer is responsible for defining the data structure. In Django, each model represents a table in the database, and the fields in each model correspond to columns in that table. The Model layer handles all database interactions, ensuring data integrity and making it easier for developers to manage and query data.
- **View**: The View layer is responsible for handling requests and returning the appropriate responses. When a user requests a page, the View processes the data, performs the necessary calculations or interactions, and then sends the processed information to the Template.

- **Template**: The Template layer is responsible for presenting data to users in a format they can understand and interact with. Templates are HTML files with placeholders for dynamic data. They define how data from the Model should be displayed to users, ensuring a separation of content and presentation.

This separation of concerns makes Django's MVT pattern highly organized and modular, allowing developers to work on different parts of the application independently and improving code maintainability.

Why Choose Django?

Django's **ease of use, scalability, security, and modular structure** make it a highly valuable framework for developers. Because Django uses Python, one of the most popular and accessible programming languages, it's also relatively easy to learn. Django's clear syntax and extensive documentation make it a great choice for both beginners and experienced developers. For companies and individual developers working on tight deadlines, Django's rapid development capabilities make it an appealing option.

Real-World Case Studies of Django Applications

Django's versatility and reliability have made it the framework of choice for several high-profile applications. Here are some notable examples:

Instagram

One of the world's most popular social media platforms, **Instagram**, uses Django to power its back end. With millions of users posting photos, videos, and stories, Instagram requires an infrastructure capable of handling massive amounts of data and high traffic. Django's scalability, coupled with its built-in security features, allows Instagram to serve this large user base efficiently and securely. The modularity of Django also makes it easier for Instagram's development team to add new features without compromising the application's overall stability.

Mozilla

Mozilla, the organization behind the Firefox browser, uses Django for several of its web applications. Mozilla values Django for its flexibility, allowing developers to create a wide range of tools and applications that support its open-source community. For Mozilla, Django's security features are also crucial, as Mozilla prioritizes privacy and security for its users.

Disqus

Disqus, a popular commenting system used by blogs and websites worldwide, is another well-known application built on Django. Disqus handles massive amounts of user-generated content daily, and Django's data handling capabilities make this possible. Django's ORM (Object-Relational Mapper) allows Disqus to manage comments, users, and moderation processes efficiently.

National Geographic and NASA

Both **National Geographic** and **NASA** use Django to manage their online content. For content-driven platforms, Django's admin interface is a significant advantage, allowing non-technical content creators and editors to manage articles, media, and other resources easily. Django's flexibility allows it to serve as a powerful content management system (CMS) capable of handling various types of content.

Smaller Projects and Startups

While large organizations often adopt Django for its power and scalability, many smaller companies and startups choose Django for its rapid development capabilities and ease of use. Startups with limited budgets and resources can leverage Django's comprehensive toolset to build robust applications quickly. For example, a small e-commerce startup can set up a product catalog, shopping cart, user authentication, and checkout system with Django's built-in modules, reducing the need for extensive custom code.

Industries Benefiting from Django

Django's versatility extends across industries. From social media and e-commerce to education and healthcare, Django provides solutions that cater to diverse requirements. Here are some specific industry applications:

- **E-commerce**: Django powers e-commerce platforms by offering customizable tools for managing product catalogs, handling orders, and processing payments.
- **Education**: Many educational platforms use Django to manage online courses, student data, and interactive learning modules.
- **Healthcare**: Django's security features make it suitable for healthcare applications that need to handle sensitive patient information.
- **Social Media and Content**: Django's scalability and support for real-time data make it ideal for social media and content-sharing platforms.

Conclusion

Django is a powerful, flexible framework that has revolutionized the way developers build web applications. By simplifying complex tasks, enhancing security, and supporting scalability, Django empowers developers to create high-quality applications for diverse needs. From small startups to tech giants like Instagram and Mozilla, Django's impact on the tech world is significant. In this book, we will explore how to harness Django's capabilities to build your own robust, scalable, and secure web applications

CHAPTER 1: INTRODUCTION TO WEB DEVELOPMENT WITH DJANGO

1. Overview of Web Development Fundamentals

To understand the context in which Django operates, let's start with an in-depth look at core web development concepts, including the client-server model, HTTP, front-end vs. back-end development, and the evolution of web frameworks.

The Client-Server Model in Detail

1. **Breaking Down the Client and Server Roles**: Discuss the client-server relationship, where clients (browsers, mobile devices) send requests to servers, which respond with the necessary data to display web content. Explain client devices in more detail, covering how different browsers interpret server data and how mobile devices handle responses differently than desktops.

2. **The Role of HTTP and HTTPS**: Explore the importance of HTTP (HyperText Transfer Protocol) in facilitating communication between client and server. Discuss HTTP methods (GET, POST, PUT, DELETE) and explain their specific roles in retrieving, creating, updating, and deleting data. Mention HTTPS (secure version) and why security is crucial in modern web applications.

3. **Additional Protocols and Data Handling**: Describe other protocols, such as WebSockets for real-time communication and WebRTC for peer-to-peer data sharing, and provide a foundation for where Django fits in supporting web standards.

Diving into Front-End vs. Back-End

1. **Front-End Essentials**: Offer insights into HTML, CSS, and JavaScript as the building blocks of front-end development. Discuss frameworks like React, Angular, and Vue, highlighting how they impact Django's usage for front-end integration and enhancing UI interactivity.

2. **Back-End Development with a Focus on Django**: Explain back-end processes like server-side scripting, database management, and authentication in more detail. Discuss how Django handles these aspects, particularly with its ORM (Object-Relational Mapper) and built-in support for SQL databases.

The Evolution of Web Development Frameworks

1. **Why Frameworks Are Essential**: Delve into the limitations of building applications from scratch (redundant code, maintenance, debugging) and how frameworks solve these

problems by providing reusable code and enforcing best practices.

2. **Comparing Django to Other Frameworks**: Offer a comparison with other frameworks like Ruby on Rails, Laravel, and Express, showing how each framework suits different development needs. Highlight Django's advantages, such as its secure defaults and scalability, and explain why it's widely adopted in the Python community.

2. What Django Is and Why It's Valuable

Django is a high-level Python web framework designed for rapid development and secure, scalable applications. This section will expand on Django's specific features, its MVT (Model-View-Template) structure, and why it's a valuable tool for web developers.

Understanding Django's "Batteries-Included" Philosophy

1. **Built-In Modules and Their Benefits**: Explain Django's "batteries-included" philosophy, where essential tools (e.g., authentication, ORM, forms, and security features) come built-in. Explore each module, showing how it saves development time by providing reliable, well-tested solutions.

2. **Security Features**: Expand on Django's security features, including CSRF protection, SQL injection protection, and user authentication. Explain why these are critical for

applications that handle sensitive data, such as e-commerce and healthcare apps.

3. **Scalability and Performance**: Discuss how Django's modular design allows applications to scale. Describe caching, database optimization, and load balancing in Django, emphasizing how it enables companies to grow their applications from prototypes to full-scale products without needing to switch frameworks.

The MVT (Model-View-Template) Structure and Its Advantages

1. **In-Depth Look at the Model Layer**: Explain how Django's Model layer interacts with databases. Discuss model fields, relationships, and validation. Provide code examples showing how Django models simplify database operations.

2. **View Layer and Request Handling**: Discuss how Django views handle incoming HTTP requests, process data, and return HTTP responses. Explain function-based and class-based views, comparing their usage and benefits with code examples.

3. **Template Layer and Presentation Logic**: Discuss how templates enable the separation of HTML content from application logic. Explain Django's template language, including filters and tags, which allow developers to format data dynamically in HTML templates.

3. Real-World Case Studies of Django Applications

To understand Django's impact and versatility, this section will cover high-profile applications built with Django and how Django empowers smaller projects.

Notable Examples of Django Applications

1. **Instagram**: Detail how Instagram leverages Django to handle its vast user base, real-time interactions, and multimedia content. Discuss Django's scalability features that support millions of daily users, and explain why Instagram relies on Django for both its security and flexibility.

2. **Mozilla**: Provide an in-depth look at how Mozilla, a leader in open-source technology, uses Django for its web applications and community support tools. Explain how Django aligns with Mozilla's values of security, openness, and user privacy.

3. **Disqus**: Examine how Disqus handles massive amounts of user comments across multiple websites using Django's data management capabilities. Discuss how Django's ORM and query optimization make it possible for Disqus to manage high volumes of real-time interactions.

Success Stories of Smaller Projects Using Django

1. **Early-Stage Startups**: Highlight examples of startups that built their initial products with Django due to its speed of development, extensive documentation, and easy-to-learn Python syntax. Explain how startups use Django to quickly launch MVPs (Minimum Viable Products) and iterate based on user feedback.

2. **Educational Platforms**: Explain how online learning platforms use Django to build course management systems, user dashboards, and live interactive features. Discuss how Django's scalability and ability to integrate with real-time communication libraries make it ideal for education-focused applications.

3. **Niche E-commerce Platforms**: Showcase small to medium-sized e-commerce websites built with Django, emphasizing Django's ability to handle product catalogs, shopping carts, and secure checkout processes. Explain how Django's customizable admin interface allows business owners to manage inventory, orders, and user profiles efficiently.

Industries Benefiting from Django's Flexibility

1. **Healthcare**: Discuss Django's use in healthcare applications, where security and data integrity are paramount. Provide

examples of HIPAA-compliant systems or patient management tools built on Django's secure foundation.

2. **Education**: Highlight Django's use in online education, where interactive and personalized content is essential. Explain how Django enables features like course tracking, content recommendations, and discussion forums that improve learning experiences.

3. **Content Management and Media**: Show how Django is used to build content-heavy platforms, supporting features like multimedia uploads, user-generated content, and real-time updates. Explain how Django's content management capabilities simplify site updates and empower non-technical content creators.

Conclusion

With its comprehensive toolset, security features, scalability, and extensive documentation, Django has become one of the most trusted frameworks for web development. From supporting early-stage startups to powering platforms like Instagram, Django proves its versatility and robustness in diverse applications. This chapter has introduced web development fundamentals, explained Django's unique advantages, and provided real-world examples to illustrate Django's capabilities.

Hands-On: This section should include plenty of code snippets, with each step building up to seeing "Hello, World!" displayed in a browser.

By the end of this chapter, readers will have a fully functioning Django setup with a basic app running locally. This chapter will empower them to feel comfortable with their environment, making the rest of the book smoother as they build more complex features.

CHAPTER 2: SETTING UP YOUR DEVELOPMENT ENVIRONMENT

Creating a smooth and efficient development environment is one of the first essential steps in Django development. The right setup not only boosts productivity but also helps prevent common issues related to dependencies, environment management, and code versioning. In this chapter, we'll explore setting up Python and Django on different operating systems, introduce virtual environments and version control, and finish with a "Hello, World!" Django app to confirm our environment is ready.

1. Setting Up Python and Django on Different Operating Systems

Django is built in Python, so having a compatible version of Python installed on your computer is a prerequisite. The setup process will vary slightly depending on your operating system, so we'll go through the steps for Windows, Mac, and Linux individually.

Python Installation

1. **Why Python Matters for Django**: Python is known for its readability, ease of use, and vast library ecosystem, which makes it an excellent language for web development. Django is compatible with Python 3, so ensure you have a recent version.

2. **Installing Python on Windows, Mac, and Linux**:

   o **Windows**:

     ▪ Download the latest Python version from python.org. During installation, select the option to "Add Python to PATH," which allows you to access Python from the command line.

     ▪ Verify the installation by opening a command prompt and typing `python --version`.

   o **Mac**:

     ▪ Use `Homebrew`, a package manager, to install Python by running `brew install python3`. Alternatively, you can download it directly from the Python website.

     ▪ Confirm the installation by running `python3 --version`.

   o **Linux**:

     ▪ Most Linux distributions come with Python pre-installed. To check, open a terminal and type `python3 --version`.

     ▪ If Python isn't installed, use the package manager for your distribution, such as `sudo apt install python3` **on** Ubuntu.

Installing Django

1. **Using `pip` to Install Django**:
   - With Python installed, you can now use `pip`, Python's package installer, to install Django. Run `pip install django` in your terminal or command prompt.
   - Confirm the installation by typing `django-admin --version`.

2. **Ensuring Compatibility**:
   - As Django releases regular updates, it's essential to ensure you're working with a compatible version of Django for this book or tutorial series. Django 3.2 and later versions are recommended due to their extended support and improvements.

2. Introduction to Virtual Environments

A virtual environment is a Python tool that helps isolate project dependencies, allowing you to create specific versions of packages for each project. This isolation ensures compatibility and prevents conflicts when working on multiple projects. Let's dive into how to create and manage virtual environments in Python.

Why Virtual Environments Are Important

1. **Dependency Management**:
   - When developing multiple projects, it's common for each project to rely on different versions of a package. Virtual environments prevent conflicts by allowing each project to maintain its dependencies separately.

2. **System Independence**:
   - With virtual environments, your project's dependencies are bundled independently of the system's global Python installation, reducing the chance of accidentally modifying or corrupting system packages.

Setting Up Virtual Environments

1. **Creating a Virtual Environment**:
   - Use Python's built-in venv module to create a virtual environment. Open a terminal and navigate to your project folder, then type:

```bash
Copy code
python -m venv myenv
```

    o   Replace `myenv` with any name you prefer for your virtual environment.

2. **Activating and Deactivating the Environment**:
   - After creating the environment, activate it using the following command:
     - **Windows**: `myenv\Scripts\activate`
     - **Mac/Linux**: `source myenv/bin/activate`
   - You should see the virtual environment's name appear in your terminal prompt, indicating it's active. When you're finished, deactivate it by typing `deactivate`.

3. **Installing Django in the Virtual Environment**:
   - With the virtual environment active, use `pip install django` to install Django only within this environment. This allows you to have multiple projects with different Django versions on the same machine.

4. **Creating a `requirements.txt` File**:
   - Use `pip freeze > requirements.txt` to generate a `requirements.txt` file that lists all packages and versions used in your project. This file makes it easy to replicate the environment later by running `pip install -r requirements.txt`.

3. Version Control with Git

Version control is essential for tracking code changes, collaborating with others, and managing multiple versions of a project. Git, one of the most widely used version control systems, enables developers to track changes in their codebase, revert to previous versions, and collaborate with others without overwriting work.

Setting Up Git

1. **Installing Git**:
   - o **Windows**: Download Git from git-scm.com and follow the installation instructions.
   - o **Mac**: Install Git via Homebrew with `brew install git`.
   - o **Linux**: Most Linux distributions come with Git pre-installed, but if not, install it with `sudo apt install git`.
2. **Configuring Git**:
   - o After installation, configure your Git username and email, which will be associated with each commit. Run:

```bash
Copy code
git config --global user.name "Your Name"
git config --global user.email
"you@example.com"
```

Essential Git Commands for Django Projects

1. **Initializing a Repository**:
   - o Navigate to your project folder and type `git init` to initialize a Git repository.
2. **Basic Git Workflow**:
   - o Use `git add` to stage changes, `git commit -m "message"` to save changes, and `git push` to upload changes to a remote repository (e.g., GitHub).
   - o Explain the importance of making regular commits with descriptive messages to keep track of changes over time.
3. **Creating a `.gitignore` File**:
   - o Certain files and folders shouldn't be tracked in version control, such as virtual environments, database files, and sensitive data. Add these to a `.gitignore` file:

```
markdown
Copy code
myenv/
*.pyc
__pycache__/
db.sqlite3
```

- o   This ensures that only essential files are included in the Git repository, keeping your project organized and secure.

4. Building Your First Django App: "Hello, World!"

With the development environment set up, it's time to build a simple Django app to ensure everything is working correctly. The following steps guide you through creating a basic "Hello, World!" app, a great way to familiarize yourself with Django's structure and functionality.

Creating a Django Project

1. **Starting a New Project**:
   - o   Inside the activated virtual environment, run the command `django-admin startproject myproject`. This will create a folder named `myproject` containing the essential files and directories Django needs to run.
2. **Understanding Django's File Structure**:
   - o   Review the files generated by Django:
     - `manage.py`: A command-line utility that lets you interact with the Django project.
     - `settings.py`: Contains configuration settings for your project, such as database settings, allowed hosts, and installed apps.

- `urls.py`: Manages the routing of URLs to the appropriate views.

Creating Your First Django App

1. **Starting a Django App**:
   o Run python manage.py startapp hello to create a new Django app called hello. The app structure will include files for models, views, and templates.

2. **Configuring the App in settings.py**:
   o Add the new app to the INSTALLED_APPS list in settings.py:

   python
   INSTALLED_APPS = [

   ...,

   'hello',

   ]

3. **Creating a Simple View**:
   o In hello/views.py, create a view function that returns a "Hello, World!" message:

   python
   from django.http import HttpResponse

   def hello_world(request):
       return HttpResponse("Hello, World!")

4. **Mapping the View to a URL**:

   o In hello/urls.py, define a URL pattern for the view. Then, include this URL pattern in the main project's urls.py:

   python

   ```
   from django.urls import path
   from . import views

   urlpatterns = [
       path('', views.hello_world, name='hello_world'),
   ]
   ```

Running the Django Development Server

1. **Starting the Server**:

   o Run `python manage.py runserver` to start the development server. Open your web browser and navigate to `http://127.0.0.1:8000/` to view your "Hello, World!" message.

2. **Understanding the Development Server's Role**:

   o The Django development server is designed for testing and development only. While it provides useful debugging information, it is not suitable for production.

3. **Troubleshooting Common Issues**:

   o List a few common issues (like port conflicts or Python path errors) and how to resolve them to ensure a smooth start with Django.

Conclusion

With your development environment set up and a "Hello, World!" app running, you now have a foundation for building Django applications. By installing Python and Django, setting up virtual environments, and familiarizing yourself with Git, you're equipped to manage projects effectively, ensure consistency, and handle dependencies efficiently. This foundational setup will save time and simplify the development process as we dive deeper into building more complex features and applications with Django in the coming chapters.

CHAPTER 3: UNDERSTANDING DJANGO'S MVT ARCHITECTURE

Django's MVT (Model-View-Template) architecture is central to how it organizes and processes web applications. This design pattern allows Django to separate concerns efficiently, making applications easier to develop, manage, and scale. In this chapter, we'll examine each MVT component, explore how it differs from the more traditional MVC (Model-View-Controller) architecture, and build a simple project to demonstrate how MVT functions in Django.

1. Introduction to MVT Architecture

Django's architecture is based on the **Model-View-Template (MVT) pattern**, a design that enables clean separation between the data layer, application logic, and presentation layer. The primary advantage of MVT is modularity, allowing developers to work on different parts of the application independently without affecting other components.

1. **Separation of Concerns**:
    - By separating models, views, and templates, Django simplifies application structure and promotes modularity. This separation makes it easier to work with each component independently, enhancing code readability and maintainability.

2. **Django's Approach to Web Applications**:

- o Django takes a "batteries-included" approach, providing built-in tools to work with each component of the MVT architecture. From models for database interactions to templates for rendering HTML, Django's MVT architecture integrates each layer seamlessly.

2. MVT vs. MVC: Understanding the Difference

Django's MVT pattern is similar to the widely known MVC (Model-View-Controller) architecture, but there's a subtle distinction. Understanding these differences is essential to grasp how Django processes requests and delivers content.

Traditional MVC Architecture

In the MVC (Model-View-Controller) architecture:

- **Model**: Manages the data and business logic. It interacts directly with the database and defines the structure of stored data.
- **View**: Manages the data representation or the user interface, displaying data as HTML, JSON, or XML.
- **Controller**: Acts as a bridge between the model and view. It processes requests, interacts with the model, and returns the correct view.

Django's MVT Architecture

In Django's MVT:

- **Model**: Just like MVC, the model in MVT handles data and interactions with the database. Models define the structure of the data, such as fields and relationships, and Django provides an ORM (Object-Relational Mapper) to simplify database operations.
- **View**: Django's views handle application logic, which processes user requests, queries data from models, and determines the response. Unlike MVC, Django views don't handle presentation directly; instead, they retrieve data and pass it to templates.
- **Template**: Django templates are responsible for presentation. They define how data should be displayed to the user, separating the front-end display from the back-end logic.

In MVC, the **Controller** takes a direct role in managing application logic and choosing the appropriate view. In Django, the view itself handles this responsibility, eliminating the need for a separate controller component. This approach simplifies request handling and reduces the complexity of the application flow.

3. Components of Django's MVT Architecture

A. Models: The Data Layer

In Django, **models** define the structure of your data. A model corresponds to a table in the database, with each attribute of the model representing a field. Django's ORM (Object-Relational Mapper) allows developers to interact with the database using Python code rather than SQL, making database operations more accessible and manageable.

1. **Creating Models**:
   - To define a model, create a Python class that inherits from django.db.models.Model. Each attribute in the class represents a field in the database table.
   - Example:

   python
   Copy code
   ```
   from django.db import models

   class Product(models.Model):
       name = models.CharField(max_length=100)
       description = models.TextField()
       price = models. Decimal Field(max _digits=10,
   decimal_ places=2)
       stock = models. Integer Field()
       Created at = models. Date Time Field (auto _now_
   add=True)
   ```

2. **Field Types and Validation**:

   o Django provides various field types (e.g., CharField, IntegerField, DecimalField, DateTimeField) to suit different data types.

   o Each field type can include validators to enforce data integrity, ensuring that data adheres to specified rules.

3. **Database Interactions**:

   o Django's ORM enables developers to create, retrieve, update, and delete records with Python code.

   o Example of interacting with the model:

   ```python
   Copy code
   # Create a new product
   product = Product(name="Laptop", description="High-performance laptop", price=1200.00, stock=10)
   product.save()

   # Retrieve a product
   product = Product. objects. get(id=1)
   ```

B. Views: The Application Logic Layer

Django **views** handle the core application logic. Views process HTTP requests, interact with the model to retrieve data, and pass the data to templates. Django provides both **function-based views** and

class-based views, allowing developers to choose the structure that best suits their needs.

1. **Function-Based Views:**

   o Function-based views (FBVs) are defined as Python functions that take a request object and return a response. FBVs are useful for simple views that don't require additional structure.

   o Example:

   python
   Copy code
   ```
   from django.http import HttpResponse
   from .models import Product


   def product_detail(request, product_id):
       product = Product.objects.get(id=product_id)
       return HttpResponse(f"Product: {product.name}, Price: ${product.price}")
   ```

2. **Class-Based Views:**

   o Class-based views (CBVs) are designed for more complex views that may require additional structure and reusability. CBVs allow developers to use Django's built-in view classes, which provide common functionalities like list views and detail views.

- o Example of a DetailView for a product:

python
Copy code
from django.views.generic import DetailView
from .models import Product

```
class ProductDetailView(DetailView):
    model = Product
    template_name = "product_detail.html"
```

3. **View Types**:
    - o Django views can be used to return different types of responses, such as HTML, JSON, or XML. This flexibility makes Django suitable for both web applications and APIs.

C. Templates: The Presentation Layer

The **template** in Django is responsible for rendering HTML content and displaying data to the user. Templates use the Django Template Language (DTL), a syntax for embedding Python expressions in HTML.

1. **Template Basics**:

o Templates are HTML files that define placeholders for dynamic data. Django uses curly braces ({{ }}) to represent variables and {% %} for logic statements (like loops or conditionals).

o Example:

html

Copy code

```
<h1>{{ product.name }}</h1>
<p>Price: ${{ product.price }}</p>
```

2. **Template Tags and Filters**:

o Template tags add logic to templates, allowing developers to include control structures (like loops) and conditionals. Template filters modify data output, such as date formatting or text transformations.

o Example of a template with tags and filters:

html

```
<h1>Product List</h1>
<ul>
    {% for product in products %}
        <li>{{    product.name    }}    -    {{
product.price|floatformat:2 }}</li>
    {% endfor %}
</ul>
```

3. **Template Inheritance**:

   o Django templates support inheritance, allowing developers to create a base template that other templates can extend. This approach is useful for defining common layout elements, like headers and footers, once and reusing them across pages.

4. Example Project: MVT in Action

Let's build a simple example project to demonstrate how each MVT component works together in Django. This example will cover the basics of creating a product listing page for an e-commerce app.

Step 1: Define the Model

1. **Create a Product Model**:

   o Define fields for product name, description, price, and stock level in models.py.

   o Run python manage.py makemigrations and python manage.py migrate to create the database table.

Step 2: Create the View

1. **Create a Product List View**:

   o Write a function-based or class-based view to retrieve all products from the database.

o Pass the list of products to the template as context data.

Example:

python
from django.shortcuts import render
from .models import Product

```
def product_list(request):
    products = Product.objects.all()
    return render(request, 'product_list.html', {'products': products})
```

Step 3: Set Up the Template

1. **Create product_list.html**:
   o Use Django template tags to display each product's name, price, and description in an HTML list.
   o Example:

html
```
<h1>Products</h1>
<ul>
    {% for product in products %}
        <li>{{ product.name }} - ${{ product.price }}</li>
```

```
{% endfor %}
</ul>
```

Step 4: Configure URL Routing

1. **Add URL Patterns**:
   - Map a URL to the product_list view in urls.py.

Example:

python

Copy code

```
from django.urls import path
from . import views

urlpatterns = [
    path('products/', views.product_list, name='product_list'),
]
```

Step 5: Test the Application

- Start the Django development server with python manage.py runserver and navigate to http://127.0.0.1:8000/products/ to view the product listing page.

5. Summary

In this chapter, we covered Django's Model-View-Template architecture and the unique role each component plays in web development. We explored the differences between MVT and MVC, detailed each MVT component, and built a simple project to illustrate how models, views, and templates work together in Django. Understanding this architecture is essential for creating scalable and maintainable applications in Django, and it provides a foundation for building more advanced features in subsequent chapters.

CHAPTER 4: CREATING AND CONFIGURING YOUR FIRST DJANGO PROJECT

Starting a new Django project is the first step toward building any Django application. In this chapter, we'll guide you through initializing a Django project, configuring the essential settings required to customize and secure your project, and setting up a reliable project structure that adheres to best practices.

1. Initializing a New Django Project

To begin, let's create a new Django project, which involves setting up the basic files and directories Django requires to function. This will establish the framework for building out the app's features and functionalities.

Step-by-Step Guide to Project Initialization

1. **Starting a Django Project with django-admin**:
   o Begin by navigating to the directory where you want to create your project, then run:

   bash
   django-admin startproject myproject

o Replace myproject with your desired project name. This command generates the essential files and directories for the project, including the main project folder and a subfolder containing configuration files.

2. **Understanding Django's Default Project Structure**:

o The command above creates the following structure:

```
markdown
myproject/
    manage.py
    myproject/
        __init__.py
        settings.py
        urls.py
        wsgi.py
        asgi.py
```

- **manage.py**: A command-line utility for managing the project (e.g., running the server, migrations).
- **settings.py**: The primary configuration file for the project, including database settings, installed applications, and security options.
- **urls.py**: Manages URL routing, defining which views should handle specific URLs.

- **wsgi.py** and **asgi.py**: Configuration files for serving the app via WSGI (Web Server Gateway Interface) or ASGI (Asynchronous Server Gateway Interface), respectively.

3. **Running the Development Server**:
   o To confirm that the project has been created correctly, run the following command:

   bash
   python manage.py runserver

   o Visit http://127.0.0.1:8000/ in your browser. You should see Django's default welcome page, indicating that the server is running and the project has been successfully initialized.

2. Configuring Essential Settings

Django provides a wide range of customizable settings in settings.py, allowing you to define everything from database configurations to security settings and time zones. Configuring these settings early on is essential for a smooth development process and secure application.

Setting Up the Database

1. **Choosing a Database**:
   - By default, Django uses SQLite, a lightweight, file-based database that's ideal for development. However, for production environments, consider switching to PostgreSQL, MySQL, or another more robust database.
   - Example configuration for PostgreSQL:

   ```python
   DATABASES = {
       'default': {
           'ENGINE': 'django.db.backends.postgresql',
           'NAME': 'mydatabase',
           'USER': 'myuser',
           'PASSWORD': 'mypassword',
           'HOST': 'localhost',
           'PORT': '5432',
       }
   }
   ```

2. **Running Initial Migrations**:
   - Django's ORM requires database tables for each installed app, which are created through migrations.

Run the following command to apply initial migrations:

bash

python manage.py migrate

o   This command creates the tables for built-in Django apps, like authentication and sessions.

Configuring Time Zone and Language

1. **Setting the Time Zone**:

   o   In settings.py, find the TIME_ZONE setting and set it to the time zone of your target audience:

   python
   Copy code
   TIME_ZONE = 'America/New_York'

   o   Django will use this time zone when managing date and time data.

2. **Setting the Language Code**:

   o   By default, Django uses English as the language, but you can change it to any supported language using the LANGUAGE_CODE setting:

python

LANGUAGE_CODE = 'en-us'

Setting Up Static and Media Files

1. **Static Files**:
   - o Static files (e.g., CSS, JavaScript) are crucial for the front end of your application. Define the STATIC_URL setting to specify the base URL for static files:

     python
     Copy code
     STATIC_URL = '/static/'

   - o Later, you can configure STATICFILES_DIRS and STATIC_ROOT for custom static file directories and collect all static files for production.

2. **Media Files**:
   - o Media files are user-uploaded content, such as profile images. In settings.py, configure the MEDIA_URL and MEDIA_ROOT settings:

     python
     Copy code
     MEDIA_URL = '/media/'
     MEDIA_ROOT = BASE_DIR / 'media'

Setting Security Configurations

1. **Secret Key**:
   - Django requires a SECRET_KEY for cryptographic signing. This key should be unique to each project and kept private. In production, consider storing it in an environment variable rather than hardcoding it in settings.py.

2. **Allowed Hosts**:
   - ALLOWED_HOSTS is a security measure that restricts which domains can serve your Django application. For local development, you can set it to an empty list, but in production, add the specific domains:

   python
   Copy code
   ```
   ALLOWED_HOSTS = ['yourdomain.com', 'www.yourdomain.com']
   ```

3. **Debug Mode**:
   - DEBUG = True enables debug mode, which shows detailed error pages in development. For production, always set DEBUG = False to prevent sensitive information from being exposed.

3. Best Practices for Project Structure and Organization

Organizing your project well from the start will save time and reduce confusion as the application grows. Django's flexibility allows for a customized project structure to suit your needs, but here are some best practices for maintaining clarity and scalability.

Using a Multi-Settings Structure

For larger projects, you might want separate settings files for development, testing, and production. A common approach is to create a settings/ folder with individual files for each environment:

1. **Creating a settings Directory**:
   o Create a settings folder inside your main project directory.
   o Move settings.py into this folder, renaming it to base.py for shared settings. Then, create development.py, production.py, and other environment-specific files.

2. **Importing Base Settings**:
   o Each environment-specific file can import the shared settings from base.py:

   python
   from .base import *

3. **Managing Secrets and Environment Variables**:
   o Use the django-environ package to manage environment variables, keeping sensitive information out of your codebase. This allows you to define secrets in an .env file and load them into your settings.

Organizing Apps and Modules

1. **Using a Modular App Structure**:
   o Django encourages breaking down functionality into apps. Each app should handle a specific feature, such as user profiles, orders, or products. This modular approach makes it easier to manage and scale features.

2. **Separating Core and Utility Apps**:
   o Divide your apps into core apps (e.g., authentication, user profiles) and utility apps (e.g., notifications, analytics). This separation helps define responsibilities and keeps related features within specific modules.

3. **Creating a Common Structure for Apps**:
   o Each app should have a consistent structure, typically including the following files:

   arduino

myapp/

    models.py

    views.py

    urls.py

    templates/

    static/

    forms.py

    admin.py

4. **Organizing Templates and Static Files**:

- o Store templates and static files in a way that mirrors your app structure. For example, place app-specific templates in a folder named after the app (myapp/templates/myapp/), making it easier to manage them as the project grows.

4. Adding Basic Apps and Functionality

To make the most of Django's modularity, we'll create a few foundational apps that can be useful in most projects. For example, an authentication app can handle user registration, login, and logout functionality.

Creating the Authentication App

1. **Starting the App**:

- o Run the following command to create an authapp for authentication:

  bash

  python manage.py startapp authapp

2. **Defining Basic Models**:
   - o Use Django's AbstractUser model to extend user profiles with additional fields, like profile_picture or bio.

3. **Setting Up Views and URLs**:
   - o Define basic views for user registration, login, and logout. Use Django's built-in authentication functions, such as LoginView and LogoutView, to manage sessions securely.

4. **Creating Templates**:
   - o Set up templates for registration and login, using Django's template tags to handle form submission and error display.

Adding Other Core Apps

1. **Product App for E-commerce Sites**:
   - o Set up a product app to handle product listings, categories, and reviews for an e-commerce site.

2. **Blog or Content App**:

o   For content-heavy sites, create a blog app to manage articles, tags, and categories.

5. Testing the Setup and Running Initial Commands

Once the project structure is established and essential configurations are in place, run a few commands to verify that everything works as expected.

Creating a Superuser

1. **Superuser Setup**:

    o   Create an admin user by running:

    bash

    python manage.py createsuperuser

    o   This user will have access to Django's admin interface, allowing you to manage database records and verify that your models work correctly.

Testing the Admin Interface

1. **Starting the Development Server**:

    o   Run python manage.py runserver and visit http://127.0.0.1:8000/admin/ to access the admin interface.

o Log in with the superuser credentials and check that all configured models appear as expected.

Testing the Initial App Configuration

1. **Testing Views and URL Routing**:
   o Visit URLs defined in each app's urls.py file to ensure that views render correctly and templates display as intended.

Conclusion

In this chapter, we've covered the foundational steps for creating and configuring a new Django project. By setting up an efficient project structure, configuring settings for security and functionality, and building a basic modular layout, you've created a solid foundation for your Django application. With this groundwork in place, you're ready to start building out more advanced features in the coming chapters, confident that your project is well-organized, secure, and optimized for growth.

CHAPTER 5: MODELS - DEFINING AND MANAGING DATA

Django's model layer is the foundation for managing application data. It allows developers to define the structure of data, interact with the database using Python code, and enforce data integrity through validation. In this chapter, we'll dive into defining models, setting up relationships between models, and applying these concepts in real-world scenarios, like creating models for a blog, user profiles, and a product catalog.

1. Introduction to Django Models

Django models are the backbone of data management, representing tables in the database and each model's attributes as fields in that table. Django's ORM (Object-Relational Mapper) allows developers to interact with these tables using Python, abstracting away raw SQL and providing a simpler interface for CRUD (Create, Read, Update, Delete) operations.

Why Models Matter in Web Applications

1. **Data Structure Definition**:
    - Models define the structure of the data and specify relationships between different types of data, such as users and products or orders and

customers. This structure helps maintain data integrity and consistency throughout the application.

2. **Simplicity and Efficiency with ORM**:

   o Django's ORM allows developers to manage data efficiently using Python code. The ORM provides built-in methods for querying, filtering, and updating data, which reduces the amount of code required to interact with the database.

Basic Model Definition

1. **Creating a Model**:

   o Each Django model is defined as a Python class that inherits from `django.db.models.Model`. The class's attributes represent database fields.

   o Example:

```python
Copy code
from django.db import models

class BlogPost(models.Model):
    title =
models.CharField(max_length=200)
    content = models.TextField()
    published_date =
models.DateTimeField(auto_now_add=True)
    author =
models.CharField(max_length=100)
```

2. **Understanding Field Types**:
   - Django provides various field types to define different kinds of data. Common fields include:
     - `CharField` for short text strings.
     - `TextField` for long text content.
     - `IntegerField` for integer numbers.
     - `DecimalField` for precise decimal numbers, useful for prices.
     - `DateTimeField` for dates and times.

3. **Model Meta Options**:
   - Django models include Meta options to customize behavior, such as specifying the database table name or ordering the records.
   - Example:

```python
Copy code
class BlogPost(models.Model):
    title =
models.CharField(max_length=200)
    # other fields

    class Meta:
        ordering = ['-published_date']  #
Sort by published date in descending
order
```

2. Defining and Managing Model Relationships

In web applications, it's common for data to be interconnected. For instance, a user might have multiple blog posts, or a product could belong to multiple categories. Django supports defining relationships between models through three primary relationship fields: `OneToOneField`, `ForeignKey`, and `ManyToManyField`.

One-to-One Relationships

1. **Using `OneToOneField`:**
   - A one-to-one relationship links one instance of a model to one instance of another model. This relationship is ideal for extending user profiles or connecting models with unique relationships.
   - Example:

   ```python
   python
   Copy code
   class UserProfile(models.Model):
       user = models.OneToOneField(User,
   on_delete=models.CASCADE)
       bio = models.TextField()
       profile_picture =
   models.ImageField(upload_to='profiles/')
   ```

2. **Real-World Use Cases:**
   - One-to-one relationships are commonly used to extend user models, creating profiles with additional data that doesn't fit in the default user model.

One-to-Many Relationships

1. **Using `ForeignKey`:**

- o A foreign key establishes a one-to-many relationship, linking one record from one model to multiple records in another. This is useful for relationships like authors and their blog posts or products within categories.
- o Example:

```python
Copy code
class Author(models.Model):
    name =
models.CharField(max_length=100)

class BlogPost(models.Model):
    author = models.ForeignKey(Author,
on_delete=models.CASCADE)
    title =
models.CharField(max_length=200)
```

2. **Foreign Key Options**:
   - o The on_delete parameter defines what happens to related records if the referenced record is deleted. Common options include:
     - CASCADE: Delete all related records.
     - SET_NULL: Set the foreign key to null.
     - PROTECT: Prevent deletion if related records exist.

Many-to-Many Relationships

1. **Using ManyToManyField**:
   - o A many-to-many relationship allows multiple records in one model to be associated with multiple records in another model. This is useful

for scenarios like tags for blog posts, where each post can have multiple tags, and each tag can belong to multiple posts.

- o Example:

```python
Copy code
class Tag(models.Model):
    name = models.CharField(max_length=50)

class BlogPost(models.Model):
    title = models.CharField(max_length=200)
    tags = models.ManyToManyField(Tag)
```

2. **Through Tables**:
   - o Django allows customization of many-to-many relationships by defining a "through" table. This table holds additional data about the relationship, such as timestamps or priority levels.

3. Real-World Examples of Models and Relationships

To solidify our understanding, let's explore three real-world scenarios where models and relationships are crucial: a blogging platform, user profiles, and an e-commerce product catalog.

Example 1: Blogging Platform

1. **Blog Post Model**:
   - o The `BlogPost` model includes fields for title, content, published date, and author, as shown in

previous examples. It has a one-to-many relationship with the author model and a many-to-many relationship with tags.

2. **Comment Model**:

   o Comments are related to individual blog posts, forming a one-to-many relationship where each post can have multiple comments.

   o Example:

```python
Copy code
class Comment(models.Model):
    post = models.ForeignKey(BlogPost,
on_delete=models.CASCADE)
    author =
models.CharField(max_length=100)
    content = models.TextField()
    created_at =
models.DateTimeField(auto_now_add=True)
```

Example 2: User Profiles with Extended Data

1. **Profile Model for Additional User Information**:

   o Extending Django's default `User` model with a one-to-one relationship to store additional information like bio, profile picture, and social links.

   o Example:

```python
Copy code
class UserProfile(models.Model):
```

```
user = models.OneToOneField(User,
on_delete=models.CASCADE)
    bio = models.TextField(blank=True)
    profile_picture =
models.ImageField(upload_to='profile_pics
/', blank=True)
    website = models.URLField(blank=True)
```

2. **Relationship to Other Models**:
   - A profile could have a many-to-many relationship with other users (for a "friends" feature) or a one-to-many relationship with posts the user has authored.

Example 3: Product Catalog for E-commerce

1. **Product Model**:
   - Products in an e-commerce site might include fields like name, description, price, SKU, and stock.
   - Example:

   ```python
   Copy code
   class Product(models.Model):
       name =
   models.CharField(max_length=100)
       description = models.TextField()
       price =
   models.DecimalField(max_digits=10,
   decimal_places=2)
       stock = models.IntegerField()
   ```

2. **Category Model and Many-to-Many Relationship**:
   - Products often belong to multiple categories, which is managed with a many-to-many relationship.

- Example:

```python
Copy code
class Category(models.Model):
    name =
models.CharField(max_length=100)

class Product(models.Model):
    name =
models.CharField(max_length=100)
    categories =
models.ManyToManyField(Category)
```

3. **Order and OrderItem Models**:
   - Orders involve a one-to-many relationship with products, managed through an intermediate model OrderItem.
   - Example:

```python
Copy code
class Order(models.Model):
    customer = models.ForeignKey(User,
on_delete=models.CASCADE)
    created_at =
models.DateTimeField(auto_now_add=True)

class OrderItem(models.Model):
    order = models.ForeignKey(Order,
on_delete=models.CASCADE)
    product = models.ForeignKey(Product,
on_delete=models.CASCADE)
    quantity =
models.PositiveIntegerField()
```

4. Managing Data with Django's ORM

With models in place, Django's ORM makes it easy to manage data using Python code. Let's explore basic ORM functions and queries for working with data.

Creating and Saving Data

1. **Creating New Records**:
   o Example:

```python
Copy code
product = Product(name="Laptop",
description="High-performance laptop",
price=1200.00, stock=10)
product.save()
```

2. **Bulk Creation**:
   o Use `bulk_create` to add multiple records at once, which improves efficiency for large datasets.

Retrieving and Filtering Data

1. **Basic Queries**:
   o `all()`, `get()`, and `filter()` methods allow you to retrieve data based on specific criteria.
   o Example:

```python
Copy code
products =
Product.objects.filter(price__gte=1000)
```

2. **Advanced Lookups**:
   o Use double underscores for complex queries, such as filtering based on related fields or dates (`price__gte`, `published_date__year=2023`).

Updating and Deleting Data

1. **Updating Records**:
   - Retrieve the record, make changes, and call `save()` to update.
   - Example:

   ```python
   Copy code
   product = Product.objects.get(id=1)
   product.price = 1300.00
   product.save()
   ```

2. **Deleting Records**:
   - Use `delete()` to remove records:

   ```python
   Copy code
   product.delete()
   ```

5. Summary

In this chapter, we explored Django models, relationships between models, and real-world examples. Django's ORM allows developers to manage data efficiently and build complex relationships between different models. With this understanding, you can now define data structures and manage them effectively in your Django application, laying the groundwork for a dynamic and interactive web experience.

CHAPTER 6: DJANGO ORM AND QUERYSETS

Django's ORM (Object-Relational Mapper) is a powerful tool that allows developers to interact with the database using Python code rather than SQL queries. The ORM abstracts the database layer, making it easier to perform complex operations while maintaining clean and readable code. In this chapter, we'll cover the basics of Django's ORM, explore QuerySets in detail, and create a simple search feature to demonstrate QuerySets in action.

1. Introduction to Django ORM

The Django ORM allows developers to interact with the database using models. With ORM, you can create, retrieve, update, and delete records in the database using Python code. This eliminates the need for SQL, providing a more intuitive way to manage data while retaining the flexibility to handle complex queries.

Benefits of Using an ORM

1. **Database Abstraction**:
   - The ORM abstracts database interactions, allowing developers to work with data without needing to write SQL. This abstraction simplifies development and allows code to be more maintainable.
2. **Cross-Database Compatibility**:
   - Django's ORM supports multiple databases (e.g., PostgreSQL, MySQL, SQLite). By using

Django's ORM, developers can switch databases without rewriting code.

3. **Data Security**:
   - o Django's ORM automatically escapes inputs to prevent SQL injection, adding an extra layer of security to data interactions.
4. **Improved Productivity**:
   - o The ORM reduces the complexity of database queries, which means developers can build applications faster, focusing on application logic rather than database operations.

2. Working with QuerySets

QuerySets are Django's way of representing a collection of database queries. A QuerySet can retrieve all records from a model or apply filters to retrieve specific records.

Creating QuerySets

1. **Basic QuerySets**:
   - o To create a QuerySet, call the model's manager method. The most common method is `objects.all()`, which retrieves all records from the table.
   - o Example:

   ```python
   python
   Copy code
   from myapp.models import Product

   products = Product.objects.all()
   ```

2. **Using the Shell for QuerySets**:

o Django's interactive shell is a great tool for experimenting with QuerySets and testing queries. Open the shell by running:

```bash
python manage.py shell
```

Filtering Data with QuerySets

1. `filter()` **Method**:
   o The `filter()` method allows you to filter records based on specific conditions.
   o Example:

```python
Copy code
products                              =
Product.objects.filter(price__gte=1000)  #
Products priced above 1000
```

2. **Using Lookup Expressions**:
   o Django provides several lookup expressions for filtering, such as:
      ▪ `exact`: Matches the exact value.
      ▪ `contains`: Searches for a substring.
      ▪ `gte`, `lte`: Greater than or equal to, less than or equal to.
   o Example:

```python
Copy code
products                              =
Product.objects.filter(name__contains="La
ptop")
```

3. **Combining Filters with AND and OR Conditions**:
   o Use multiple filters to combine conditions with AND. To combine filters with OR, use Q objects.
   o Example:

```
python
Copy code
from django.db.models import Q

# Products that are laptops or priced over
1000
products                                    =
Product.objects.filter(Q(name__contains="
Laptop") | Q(price__gte=1000))
```

Sorting and Ordering Data

1. `order_by()` **Method**:
   - Use `order_by()` to sort results by a specific field. Prefix the field name with a minus sign (-) to sort in descending order.
   - Example:

   ```
   python
   Copy code
   products                                    =
   Product.objects.all().order_by('-price')
   ```

2. **Multiple Fields in** `order_by()`:
   - You can sort by multiple fields by passing a list of field names.
   - Example:

   ```
   python
   Copy code
   products                                    =
   Product.objects.all().order_by('category'
   , '-price')
   ```

Limiting and Slicing QuerySets

1. **Using Array-Like Slicing**:
   - QuerySets can be sliced using array-like indexing to limit results.
   - Example:

```python
Copy code
# Get the first 10 products
products = Product.objects.all()[:10]
```

2. **Using `first()` and `last()` Methods**:
   - Use `first()` and `last()` to retrieve the first or last object in a QuerySet.
   - Example:

```python
Copy code
latest_product                          =
Product.objects.order_by('-
created_at').first()
```

3. QuerySet Methods and Aggregations

Django's ORM includes powerful methods to aggregate and annotate data, allowing you to perform calculations directly in the database.

Aggregations with `aggregate()`

1. **Common Aggregation Functions**:
   - Django provides aggregation functions like `Sum`, `Avg`, `Min`, and `Max` for calculating summary data.
   - Example:

```python
Copy code
from django.db.models import Avg

avg_price                                =
Product.objects.aggregate(Avg('price'))
```

2. **Multiple Aggregations in a Single Query**:

- o You can use multiple aggregations in a single `aggregate()` call.
- o Example:

```python
Copy code
from django.db.models import Min, Max

stats                                       =
Product.objects.aggregate(min_price=Min('
price'), max_price=Max('price'))
```

Annotating Data with `annotate()`

1. **Using `annotate()` for Calculated Fields**:
   - o `annotate()` adds calculated fields to each record in the QuerySet. This is useful for calculations like total prices in an order or average ratings.
   - o Example:

```python
Copy code
from django.db.models import Count

categories                                   =
Product.objects.values('category').annota
te(product_count=Count('id'))
```

2. **Combining Aggregation with Filtering**:
   - o You can combine `annotate()` with filtering to calculate values for specific subsets of data.
   - o Example:

```python
Copy code
popular_products                             =
Product.objects.annotate(order_count=Coun
t('order')).filter(order_count__gte=5)
```

Complex Queries with Subqueries and Expressions

1. **Using Subqueries**:
   - Django's ORM supports subqueries to retrieve related data. This is useful for complex queries where the results depend on another table.
   - Example:

   ```python
   Copy code
   from django.db.models import OuterRef,
   Subquery

   recent_order =
   Order.objects.filter(product=OuterRef('pk
   ')).order_by('-created_at')
   products =
   Product.objects.annotate(latest_order_dat
   e=Subquery(recent_order.values('created_a
   t')[:1]))
   ```

2. **Expressions for Arithmetic Operations**:
   - Expressions allow you to perform arithmetic operations within queries, such as adjusting prices or calculating discounts.
   - Example:

   ```python
   Copy code
   from django.db.models import F

   # Increase all product prices by 10%
   Product.objects.update(price=F('price') *
   1.1)
   ```

4. Case Study: Building a Search Feature with QuerySets

Let's apply the concepts learned in this chapter by building a search feature for an e-commerce application. We'll create a function that allows users to search for products by name, category, and price range.

Setting Up the Search View

1. **Defining the Search Function**:
   - Create a search view in `views.py` that accepts query parameters for `name`, `category`, `min_price`, and `max_price`.
   - Example:

```python
Copy code
from django.shortcuts import render
from .models import Product

def product_search(request):
    products = Product.objects.all()
    query = request.GET.get('q')
    if query:
        products =
products.filter(name__icontains=query)
    return render(request,
'product_search.html', {'products':
products})
```

2. **Adding Filters for Category and Price Range**:
   - Update the search view to include filters for category and price range based on user input.
   - Example:

```python
Copy code
def product_search(request):
    products = Product.objects.all()
    query = request.GET.get('q')
    min_price =
request.GET.get('min_price')
    max_price =
request.GET.get('max_price')
```

```
        category =
request.GET.get('category')

        if query:
            products =
products.filter(name__icontains=query)
        if category:
            products =
products.filter(category__name=category)
        if min_price:
            products =
products.filter(price__gte=min_price)
        if max_price:
            products =
products.filter(price__lte=max_price)

        return render(request,
'product_search.html', {'products':
products})
```

Creating the Search Form in the Template

1. **Building the Search Form**:
   o In `product_search.html`, create a form with fields for the search query, category, and price range.
   o Example:

   ```html
   Copy code
   <form method="get" action="{% url
   'product_search' %}">
       <input type="text" name="q"
   placeholder="Search products">
       <input type="number" name="min_price"
   placeholder="Min price">
       <input type="number" name="max_price"
   placeholder="Max price">
       <button type="submit">Search</button>
   </form>
   ```

2. **Displaying Search Results**:

- o After running the query, display the filtered products with a loop in the template.
- o Example:

```html
Copy code
<ul>
    {% for product in products %}
        <li>{{ product.name }} - ${{
product.price }}</li>
    {% endfor %}
</ul>
```

Testing the Search Feature

1. **Testing Edge Cases**:
   - o Test the search with different combinations of inputs, such as only name, only price range, and combinations to ensure that the filters work as expected.
2. **Handling Empty Search Results**:
   - o Display a message in the template when no products match the search criteria.

5. Summary

In this chapter, we explored Django's ORM, covering how to use QuerySets to create, retrieve, and manipulate data efficiently. We also walked through advanced QuerySet methods, including filtering, ordering, and aggregating data, and built a search feature for an e-commerce application to demonstrate QuerySets in action. With a solid understanding of QuerySets, you're now equipped to handle complex data queries in Django, making your application more dynamic and responsive to user needs.

CHAPTER 7: CREATING VIEWS AND URLS

Django views are the heart of application logic, processing HTTP requests and rendering responses. Combined with URL routing, views enable dynamic interactions between users and the application. In this chapter, we'll delve into the basics of Django views, learn about URL configurations, and walk through a practical example of routing requests in a multi-page app.

1. Introduction to Django Views

In Django, views are Python functions or classes that handle HTTP requests and return HTTP responses. Views are the middle layer of Django's Model-View-Template (MVT) architecture, interacting with models to retrieve or modify data and passing that data to templates for rendering.

Types of Django Views

1. **Function-Based Views (FBVs)**:
   - Function-based views are simple Python functions that accept an `HttpRequest` object and return an `HttpResponse` object. They're ideal for straightforward view logic that doesn't require additional structure.
   - Example of a function-based view:

```python
Copy code
from django.http import HttpResponse

def hello_world(request):
    return HttpResponse("Hello, World!")
```

2. **Class-Based Views (CBVs)**:
   - Class-based views provide more structure and reusable functionality, especially for complex views. Django's CBVs offer generic views, like `DetailView`, `ListView`, `CreateView`, etc., which simplify common tasks like displaying lists or creating new records.
   - Example of a class-based view:

```python
Copy code
from        django.views.generic        import
TemplateView

class HomePageView(TemplateView):
    template_name = "home.html"
```

3. **Choosing Between FBVs and CBVs**:
   - Use FBVs for simple views with straightforward logic.
   - Use CBVs for complex views that benefit from built-in functionality or require reusable structures.

2. URL Routing and Configuration

URL routing in Django directs incoming requests to the appropriate views based on URL patterns. The `urls.py` file in each Django app defines which URLs should trigger which views.

Understanding URL Patterns

1. **Setting Up URL Patterns**:
   - URL patterns are defined using Django's `path()` function, which associates a URL with a specific view. Each URL pattern includes a route, a view, and an optional name.
   - Example:

```python
Copy code
from django.urls import path
from . import views

urlpatterns = [
    path('', views.home, name='home'),
    path('about/',                views.about,
name='about'),
]
```

2. **Capturing URL Parameters**:
   - URL patterns can capture parameters from the URL, passing them as arguments to the view. This is useful for dynamic content, such as viewing specific blog posts or products.
   - Example:

```python
Copy code
path('post/<int:post_id>/',
views.post_detail, name='post_detail')
```

3. **Including URLs from Other Apps**:
   - For modularity, Django allows each app to have its own `urls.py` file, which can then be included in the main project's `urls.py`. This helps organize URL configurations in larger projects.
   - Example in `project/urls.py`:

```python
Copy code
from django.urls import path, include
```

```
urlpatterns = [
    path('blog/', include('blog.urls')),
]
```

3. Function-Based Views in Depth

Function-based views offer flexibility and simplicity, making them ideal for basic to moderately complex view logic. Let's explore how to build and structure FBVs effectively.

Basic Function-Based View

1. **Creating a Simple View**:
   - A basic FBV takes a `request` parameter and returns an HTTP response. You can return text using `HttpResponse` or render HTML templates using Django's `render()` function.
   - Example:

   ```python
   Copy code
   from django.shortcuts import render

   def home(request):
       return render(request, 'home.html')
   ```

Handling Data and Rendering Templates

1. **Passing Context to Templates**:
   - To send data to a template, use Django's `render()` function with a context dictionary.
   - Example:

   ```python
   Copy code
   def home(request):
   ```

```
        context  =  {'title':  'Welcome  to  the
Home Page'}
        return   render(request,   'home.html',
context)
```

2. Handling Form Submissions in FBVs:

- o Use FBVs to handle GET and POST requests, which are common in forms. For example, a form view can handle both displaying the form (GET) and processing the submitted data (POST).
- o Example:

```python
Copy code
from django.shortcuts import redirect

def submit_form(request):
    if request.method == "POST":
        name = request.POST.get("name")
        # Process form data
        return redirect('home')
    return render(request, 'form.html')
```

Using Decorators with FBVs

1. Adding Permissions with Decorators:

- o Decorators, like @login_required, can restrict access to views based on user status or permissions.
- o Example:

```python
Copy code
from django.contrib.auth.decorators import login_required

@login_required
def dashboard(request):
    return                 render(request,
'dashboard.html')
```

2. **Custom Decorators**:
   - You can create custom decorators for specific functionality, like verifying user roles or enforcing specific conditions.

4. Class-Based Views in Depth

Class-based views (CBVs) in Django provide built-in view classes that simplify common tasks, such as rendering templates, displaying lists, or handling forms.

Working with Generic CBVs

1. **TemplateView**:
   - `TemplateView` renders a specified template without requiring additional logic, ideal for static pages like "About" or "Contact."
   - Example:

   ```python
   Copy code
   from django.views.generic import TemplateView

   class AboutView(TemplateView):
       template_name = "about.html"
   ```

2. **ListView and DetailView**:
   - `ListView` displays a list of objects from a model, while `DetailView` shows details for a single object. These views are helpful for displaying dynamic content, such as lists of blog posts or products.
   - Example:

   ```python
   Copy code
   ```

```
from django.views.generic import ListView,
DetailView
from .models import Product

class ProductListView(ListView):
    model = Product
    template_name = "product_list.html"

class ProductDetailView(DetailView):
    model = Product
    template_name = "product_detail.html"
```

3. **CreateView, UpdateView, and DeleteView**:
   o These views handle form processing and CRUD
     (Create, Read, Update, Delete) operations. They
     are useful for managing data, such as adding or
     editing products in an admin panel.
   o Example:

```
python
Copy code
from    django.views.generic.edit    import
CreateView
from .models import Product

class ProductCreateView(CreateView):
    model = Product
    fields   =   ['name',   'description',
'price']
    template_name = "product_form.html"
```

Customizing CBVs with Methods and Attributes

1. **Overriding Default Methods**:
   o CBVs provide methods like `get_context_data()`
     and `form_valid()` that can be overridden for
     custom functionality.
   o Example:

```
python
Copy code
```

```
class ProductListView(ListView):
    model = Product
    template_name = "product_list.html"

    def get_context_data(self, **kwargs):
        context                              =
super().get_context_data(**kwargs)
        context['extra_data']    =    'Some
Extra Data'
        return context
```

2. **Mixing FBV and CBV Logic**:
   o Use CBVs for base functionality and extend them with custom methods to suit specific needs.

5. Real-World Example: Routing Requests in a Multi-Page App

To understand views and URLs in action, let's create a multi-page application with a homepage, product list, product detail, and contact page.

Step 1: Define URLs and Views

1. **Setting Up URL Patterns**:
   o Define URL patterns for each page in `urls.py`, associating them with specific views.
   o Example:

```python
Copy code
from django.urls import path
from . import views

urlpatterns = [
    path('', views.HomePageView.as_view(),
name='home'),
```

```
    path('products/',
views.ProductListView.as_view(),
name='product_list'),
    path('products/<int:pk>/',
views.ProductDetailView.as_view(),
name='product_detail'),
    path('contact/',
views.ContactView.as_view(),
name='contact'),
]
```

2. **Creating Views for Each Page**:
   o Use a combination of FBVs and CBVs to define views for each page.
   o Example:

   ```python
   Copy code
   from django.views.generic import ListView,
   DetailView, TemplateView
   from .models import Product

   class HomePageView(TemplateView):
       template_name = "home.html"

   class ProductListView(ListView):
       model = Product
       template_name = "product_list.html"

   class ProductDetailView(DetailView):
       model = Product
       template_name = "product_detail.html"
   ```

Step 2: Setting Up the Contact Page with a Form

1. **Creating a Contact Form**:
   o Define a form to handle user input on the contact page. This form might include fields like name, email, and message.
   o Example form class:

   ```python
   ```

```
Copy code
from django import forms

class ContactForm(forms.Form):
    name = forms.CharField(max_length=100)
    email = forms.EmailField()
    message                          =
forms.CharField(widget=forms.Textarea)
```

2. **Handling Form Submission in the Contact View**:
   - Create a view to handle both the GET (display form) and POST (process submission) requests.
   - Example:

```python
python
Copy code
from django.shortcuts import render
from .forms import ContactForm

def contact(request):
    if request.method == "POST":
        form = ContactForm(request.POST)
        if form.is_valid():
            # Process form data
            return redirect('home')
    else:
        form = ContactForm()
    return render(request, 'contact.html',
{'form': form})
```

Step 3: Linking Pages Together

1. **Using URL Names in Templates**:
   - In each template, use `{% url %}` to link to other pages by URL name, ensuring a maintainable and flexible navigation structure.
   - Example in `home.html`:

```html
html
Copy code
<a href="{% url 'product_list' %}">View
Products</a>
```

```
<a href="{% url 'contact' %}">Contact
Us</a>
```

2. **Testing Navigation**:
    o   Check that each page links to the others
        correctly and that URLs are resolving as
        expected.

6. Summary

In this chapter, we covered the basics of Django views and URL
routing, explored the differences between function-based and class-
based views, and walked through building a multi-page application
with views for different pages. Understanding how to create views
and route URLs is essential for making Django applications
interactive and accessible to users. This foundation will be crucial
as we add more features and enhance interactivity in the following
chapters.

CHAPTER 9: FORMS AND USER INPUT

Forms are a fundamental part of web applications, enabling user interactions, data submissions, and dynamic updates. Django simplifies form handling by providing a robust forms framework that makes it easy to validate user input and store data in the database. In this chapter, we'll dive into creating and processing forms, handling validation and user feedback, and build registration and login forms as a practical example.

1. Introduction to Django Forms

Django forms streamline the process of creating, validating, and processing user input. With Django's forms framework, developers can easily handle complex data validation and error handling, ensuring that only valid data reaches the database.

Benefits of Using Django Forms

1. **Built-In Validation**:
   - Django forms include automatic validation for standard field types (e.g., email, date), simplifying data integrity and error handling.
2. **Automatic HTML Generation**:
   - Django forms can generate HTML form elements, ensuring consistent styling and structure across forms.
3. **Security**:

- o Django's forms framework automatically protects against common vulnerabilities, such as Cross-Site Request Forgery (CSRF).

2. Creating and Processing Django Forms

Django forms can be created in several ways, including using form classes (`forms.Form` and `forms.ModelForm`) and manually building HTML forms. Each method has advantages, depending on the complexity and requirements of the form.

Creating a Simple Form with `forms.Form`

1. **Defining a Basic Form**:
   - o The `forms.Form` class allows you to create custom forms by defining fields, which can be text inputs, dates, checkboxes, etc.
   - o Example:

   ```python
   python
   Copy code
   from django import forms

   class ContactForm(forms.Form):
       name = forms.CharField(max_length=100)
       email = forms.EmailField()
       message                              =
   forms.CharField(widget=forms.Textarea)
   ```

2. **Rendering the Form in a Template**:
   - o To display the form, pass it from the view to the template and use `{{ form.as_p }}` to render each field wrapped in `<p>` tags.
   - o Example:

   ```html
   html
   Copy code
   ```

```
<form method="post">
    {% csrf_token %}
    {{ form.as_p }}
    <button type="submit">Submit</button>
</form>
```

Using `forms.ModelForm` for Database-Driven Forms

1. **Defining a ModelForm**:
   - `ModelForm` is a subclass of `forms.Form` that automatically generates form fields based on a Django model. This is ideal for forms that save data directly to the database.
   - Example:

   ```python
   Copy code
   from django import forms
   from .models import Product

   class ProductForm(forms.ModelForm):
       class Meta:
           model = Product
           fields = ['name', 'description', 'price']
   ```

2. **Rendering a ModelForm**:
   - Like regular forms, ModelForms can be rendered in templates using `{{ form.as_p }}`, or you can customize the layout by rendering each field individually.

Customizing Form Fields

1. **Adding Labels, Help Text, and Widgets**:
   - Customize each field by specifying `label`, `help_text`, or `widget` attributes.
   - Example:

```python
class ProductForm(forms.ModelForm):
    class Meta:
        model = Product
        fields = ['name', 'description', 'price']
        widgets = {
            'description':
forms.Textarea(attrs={'rows': 4}),
            }
        labels = {
            'name': 'Product Name',
            }
        help_texts = {
            'price': 'Enter the product price in USD',
            }
```

2. **Custom Validation**:
   o Use `clean_<fieldname>()` methods for field-specific validation and `clean()` for form-wide validation.

3. Handling Form Validation and User Feedback

Form validation is essential to ensure data integrity and guide users when they enter incorrect or incomplete data. Django provides automatic validation for basic fields and allows you to add custom validation.

Built-In Validation

1. **Field-Level Validation**:
   o Django fields (e.g., `EmailField`, `URLField`, `DateField`) include built-in validation. If invalid data is entered, Django automatically raises validation errors and displays them in the form.
   o Example:

```python
Copy code
email                                    =
forms.EmailField(error_messages={'invalid
': 'Please enter a valid email address.'})
```

2. **Required Fields**:
   o By default, fields are required. Use `required=False` to make a field optional.

Custom Validation

1. **Field-Specific Validation**:
   o To validate a specific field, define a `clean_<fieldname>()` method in the form class.
   o Example:

```python
Copy code
class ContactForm(forms.Form):
    name = forms.CharField(max_length=100)
    email = forms.EmailField()

    def clean_email(self):
        email                            =
self.cleaned_data.get('email')
        if                              not
email.endswith('@example.com'):
            raise
forms.ValidationError("Please use an email
from example.com")
        return email
```

2. **Form-Wide Validation**:
   o To validate fields in combination, use the `clean()` method to perform form-wide validation.
   o Example:

```python
class SignupForm(forms.Form):
```

```
    password                        =
forms.CharField(widget=forms.PasswordInpu
t)
    confirm_password                =
forms.CharField(widget=forms.PasswordInpu
t)

    def clean(self):
        cleaned_data = super().clean()
        password                     =
cleaned_data.get("password")
        confirm_password             =
cleaned_data.get("confirm_password")

        if password != confirm_password:
            raise
forms.ValidationError("Passwords  do  not
match.")
```

Displaying Error Messages

1. **Error Handling in Templates**:
    o   Django automatically attaches error messages
        to each form field, which can be displayed in
        templates.
    o   Example:

```html
html
<div>
    {{ form.non_field_errors }}
    {% for field in form %}
        <p>{{ field.label }}: {{ field
}}</p>
        {% if field.errors %}
            <ul>
                {%      for     error    in
field.errors %}
                    <li>{{ error }}</li>
                {% endfor %}
            </ul>
        {% endif %}
    {% endfor %}
</div>
```

101

2. **Customizing Error Messages**:
   - Customize error messages for each field by defining `error_messages` for validation.

4. Real-World Example: Building Registration and Login Forms

Let's apply what we've learned to build user registration and login forms, two essential components of most web applications.

Step 1: Creating a Registration Form

1. **Defining the Registration Form**:
   - Create a `RegistrationForm` with fields for username, email, password, and confirm_password.
   - Example:

```python
from django import forms
from django.contrib.auth.models import User

class RegistrationForm(forms.ModelForm):
    password = forms.CharField(widget=forms.PasswordInput)
    confirm_password = forms.CharField(widget=forms.PasswordInput)

    class Meta:
        model = User
        fields = ['username', 'email', 'password']

    def clean(self):
        cleaned_data = super().clean()
        password = cleaned_data.get('password')
```

```
        confirm_password              =
cleaned_data.get('confirm_password')

        if password != confirm_password:
            raise
forms.ValidationError("Passwords   do   not
match.")
```

2. Creating the Registration View:

- o In `views.py`, **define a view to handle form submission, saving a new user if the form is valid.**
- o **Example:**

```python
Copy code
from   django.shortcuts   import   render,
redirect
from   django.contrib.auth.models   import
User
from .forms import RegistrationForm

def register(request):
    if request.method == "POST":
        form                          =
RegistrationForm(request.POST)
        if form.is_valid():
            user = form.save(commit=False)

user.set_password(form.cleaned_data['pass
word'])
            user.save()
            return redirect('login')
    else:
        form = RegistrationForm()
    return                  render(request,
'register.html', {'form': form})
```

3. Rendering the Registration Form in a Template:

- o **Create a** `register.html` **template and render the form.**
- o **Example:**

```html
Copy code
<form method="post">
    {% csrf_token %}
    {{ form.as_p }}
    <button
type="submit">Register</button>
</form>
```

Step 2: Building a Login Form

1. **Creating a Login Form**:
   - Use Django's built-in `AuthenticationForm`, which handles username and password authentication.
   - Example:

```python
Copy code
from django.contrib.auth.forms import
AuthenticationForm

def login_view(request):
    if request.method == "POST":
        form = AuthenticationForm(request,
data=request.POST)
        if form.is_valid():
            # Authenticate and log in the
user
            return redirect('home')
    else:
        form = AuthenticationForm()
    return render(request, 'login.html',
{'form': form})
```

2. **Rendering the Login Form in a Template**:
   - Create a `login.html` template with the form.
   - Example:

```html
<form method="post">
    {% csrf_token %}
```

```
{{ form.as_p }}
<button type="submit">Login</button>
</form>
```

3. **Handling Authentication**:
    o   Use Django's built-in authentication views and the `login()` function to log in users. You can also redirect authenticated users to different pages based on conditions.

Step 3: Redirecting and Providing Feedback

1. **Redirecting After Successful Login/Registration**:
    o   Use `redirect()` to send users to the appropriate page after successful registration or login.
2. **Displaying Feedback Messages**:
    o   Use Django's `messages` framework to provide feedback messages on actions like successful login or form submission errors.
    o   Example:

```python
python
Copy code
from django.contrib import messages

def register(request):
    if form.is_valid():
        # After saving user
        messages.success(request,
'Registration successful!')
        return redirect('login')
```

5. Summary

In this chapter, we covered Django forms, including how to create custom forms and ModelForms, handle validation, and display error messages. We built a user registration and login system as a real-world example, demonstrating form handling and user feedback. Mastering Django forms and user input will allow you to build interactive, user-friendly applications that handle data input securely and effectively.

CHAPTER 9: DJANGO TEMPLATES AND RENDERING HTML

Django's templating system is designed to help developers build dynamic, data-driven HTML templates that interact with Django's backend. Django's templating language (DTL) simplifies the process of embedding data and logic into HTML, enabling you to create user-friendly interfaces. In this chapter, we'll cover the basics of Django templates, explore template inheritance, and build a responsive front end using CSS frameworks like Bootstrap or TailwindCSS.

1. Introduction to Django Templates

Django templates are HTML files with embedded placeholders that allow you to display dynamic content. The Django Template Language (DTL) is designed to separate application logic from presentation, helping you keep your code organized and maintainable.

Why Use Django Templates?

1. **Separation of Concerns**:
    o Templates keep the presentation layer separate from application logic, allowing frontend and backend code to remain modular and organized.
2. **Dynamic Content**:
    o With Django templates, you can easily render data-driven pages. Templates allow you to

dynamically load data from the database, personalize content for users, and customize views based on user input.

3. **Ease of Use**:
   - DTL is intuitive and easy to learn, with basic syntax for loops, conditionals, and filters that make it easy to customize content.

2. Django Template Language (DTL) Basics

Django's template language provides a range of syntax elements to render data dynamically, including variables, template tags, and filters.

Using Variables in Templates

1. **Embedding Variables**:
   - Use double curly braces ({{ }}) to insert variables into templates. These variables can be passed from views and rendered in the HTML.
   - Example:

   ```html
   Copy code
   <h1>Welcome, {{ user.username }}!</h1>
   ```

2. **Accessing Model Fields**:
   - When passing model instances to templates, you can access model fields directly using dot notation.
   - Example:

   ```html
   Copy code
   <p>{{ product.name }} - ${{ product.price }}</p>
   ```

Template Tags

1. **Loops**:
   - The `{% for %}` tag allows you to loop through lists and display each item, making it essential for lists like product catalogs or blog posts.
   - Example:

   ```html
   Copy code
   <ul>
       {% for product in products %}
           <li>{{  product.name  }}  -  ${{ product.price }}</li>
       {% endfor %}
   </ul>
   ```

2. **Conditionals**:
   - The `{% if %}` tag allows you to render content based on conditions.
   - Example:

   ```html
   Copy code
   {% if user.is_authenticated %}
       <p>Welcome, {{ user.username }}!</p>
   {% else %}
       <p>Please log in to continue.</p>
   {% endif %}
   ```

Template Filters

1. **Using Filters to Modify Output**:
   - Filters allow you to modify variables in templates. Common filters include `date`, `length`, `lower`, `upper`, and `truncatewords`.
   - Example:

```html
Copy code
<p>{{ product.description|truncatewords:20
}}</p>
```

2. **Custom Filters**:
    - You can create custom filters to apply specific transformations to template data.

3. Template Inheritance and Reusability

Django's template inheritance system allows you to create a base layout that other templates can extend. This approach enables reusability and consistency, as common elements like headers and footers can be defined once and reused across multiple templates.

Creating a Base Template

1. **Defining a Base Structure**:
    - Create a base template that includes the overall structure, such as headers, navigation, and footers. Use {% block %} tags for sections that will change on each page.
    - Example (base.html):

```html
Copy code
<!DOCTYPE html>
<html lang="en">
<head>
    <title>{% block title %}My Site{% endblock %}</title>
</head>
<body>
    <header>
        <h1>Welcome to My Site</h1>
    </header>
    <nav>
```

```
        <a     href="{%     url     'home'
%}">Home</a>
        <a     href="{%     url     'about'
%}">About</a>
    </nav>
    <main>
        {% block content %}{% endblock %}
    </main>
    <footer>
        <p>&copy; 2024 My Site</p>
    </footer>
</body>
</html>
```

2. **Extending the Base Template**:
   o Other templates can extend `base.html` and fill in the content for each block, such as `title` and `content`.
   o **Example** (`home.html`):

```html
Copy code
{% extends "base.html" %}

{% block title %}Home{% endblock %}

{% block content %}
    <h2>Homepage</h2>
    <p>Welcome to the homepage!</p>
{% endblock %}
```

Benefits of Template Inheritance

1. **Consistent Layout**:
   o Template inheritance ensures a consistent layout across the site, making updates to headers, footers, or navigation simpler and more efficient.
2. **Improved Maintenance**:

o   Since you only need to update the base
    template to make layout changes, maintaining a
    consistent design is easier.

4. Rendering Dynamic Content with Views

Views play an essential role in passing data to templates. Data passed from views can include model instances, lists, or context variables.

Passing Context Data to Templates

1. **Using `render()`:**
    o   In Django, the `render()` function is commonly
        used to render templates with context data.
    o   Example:

    ```python
    Copy code
    from django.shortcuts import render
    from .models import Product

    def product_list(request):
        products = Product.objects.all()
        return                     render(request,
    'product_list.html',              {'products':
    products})
    ```

2. **Accessing Context Data in Templates:**
    o   The data passed in the context dictionary can be
        accessed directly in the template using variable
        names.

Using Template Context Processors

1. **What Are Context Processors?**:
   - Context processors are functions that inject additional data into every template. For example, the `user` object is accessible in every template because of the `auth` context processor.
2. **Adding Custom Context Processors**:
   - Create custom context processors to pass specific data (e.g., global settings) to all templates.

5. Styling with Bootstrap or TailwindCSS

CSS frameworks like Bootstrap and TailwindCSS provide pre-built styling and components, making it easy to create responsive and visually appealing pages.

Integrating Bootstrap

1. **Adding Bootstrap to Your Project**:
   - Include Bootstrap's CSS and JavaScript by adding the CDN links to your base template's `<head>` and `<body>` sections.
   - Example:

```html
Copy code
<head>
    <link
href="https://cdn.jsdelivr.net/npm/bootst
rap@5.3.0/dist/css/bootstrap.min.css"
rel="stylesheet">
</head>
```

2. **Using Bootstrap Components**:

- o Utilize Bootstrap classes and components, such as grids, navigation bars, buttons, and modals, to enhance the layout.
- o Example:

```html
Copy code
<div class="container">
    <h1 class="text-primary">Welcome to My
Site</h1>
    <button class="btn btn-success">Learn
More</button>
</div>
```

Integrating TailwindCSS

1. **Adding TailwindCSS**:
   - o Include TailwindCSS using a CDN link or install it via npm for a more customized setup.
   - o Example:

```html
Copy code
<head>
    <link
href="https://cdn.jsdelivr.net/npm/tailwi
ndcss@2.0.0/dist/tailwind.min.css"
rel="stylesheet">
</head>
```

2. **Using Utility Classes for Styling**:
   - o TailwindCSS offers utility classes for styling elements without writing custom CSS. This approach allows for rapid customization and responsive design.
   - o Example:

```html
Copy code
<div class="container mx-auto p-4">
```

```
<h1  class="text-3xl  font-bold  text-
blue-600">Welcome to My Site</h1>
    <button class="bg-green-500 text-white
px-4 py-2 rounded">Learn More</button>
</div>
```

6. Real-World Example: Building a Responsive Product Page

Let's create a responsive product listing page for an e-commerce site, using Django templates and Bootstrap or TailwindCSS for styling.

Step 1: Define the View and URL

1. **Create the Product View:**
   - Define a view to retrieve products and pass them to the template.
   - Example:

   ```python
   python
   Copy code
   from django.shortcuts import render
   from .models import Product

   def product_list(request):
       products = Product.objects.all()
       return              render(request,
   'product_list.html',        {'products':
   products})
   ```

2. **Define the URL Pattern:**
   - Add the URL pattern for the product page in urls.py.
   - Example:

   ```python
   python
   Copy code
   from django.urls import path
   from . import views
   ```

```
urlpatterns = [
    path('products/', views.product_list,
name='product_list'),
]
```

Step 2: Create the Template

1. **Set Up** `product_list.html`:
   - o Extend a base template and create the product list layout.
   - o Example:

```html
Copy code
{% extends "base.html" %}

{% block content %}
    <div class="container">
        <h2>Our Products</h2>
        <div class="row">
            {% for product in products %}
                <div class="col-md-4">
                    <div class="card mb-
4">
                        <img src="{{
product.image.url }}" class="card-img-top"
alt="{{ product.name }}">
                        <div class="card-
body">
                            <h5
class="card-title">{{ product.name }}</h5>
                            <p
class="card-text">${{ product.price }}</p>
                            <a href="#"
class="btn btn-primary">View Details</a>
                        </div>
                    </div>
                </div>
            {% endfor %}
        </div>
    </div>
{% endblock %}
```

2. **Adding Responsive Design**:
   o The Bootstrap grid system ensures the product layout is responsive, adjusting to different screen sizes automatically.

7. Summary

In this chapter, we covered Django templates and the Django Template Language (DTL) for rendering dynamic HTML. We explored template inheritance to create a reusable layout structure, passed data from views to templates, and integrated CSS frameworks like Bootstrap or TailwindCSS to build a responsive product page. Mastering Django templates and rendering will enable you to create user-friendly interfaces that enhance the overall experience of your Django application.

CHAPTER 10: AUTHENTICATION AND USER MANAGEMENT

User authentication and management are critical components of most web applications, especially those requiring personalized content or restricting access to certain pages. Django offers a robust built-in authentication system to manage user accounts securely and efficiently. In this chapter, we'll explore Django's authentication framework, create registration and login systems, handle password management, and implement access control with roles and permissions.

1. Introduction to Django's Authentication System

Django's authentication system includes tools for user registration, login, logout, and permission management. These built-in functionalities provide secure methods for managing user sessions and access, allowing developers to focus on building features rather than implementing authentication from scratch.

Key Components of Django's Authentication System

1. **User Model**:
   - Django's default `User` model includes essential fields like username, password, email, and permissions.
   - The model can be customized or extended using a custom user model or by creating a `UserProfile` model.

2. **Authentication Views**:
   - o Django provides built-in views for login, logout, and password reset, simplifying the process of setting up authentication flows.
3. **Sessions**:
   - o Django's session framework keeps track of user login status and enables features like personalized content and restricted access to specific views.
4. **Permissions and Groups**:
   - o Permissions allow you to control access to certain parts of the application. Groups make it easy to assign permissions to multiple users with similar roles.

2. User Registration

User registration allows new users to create accounts, setting the foundation for a personalized experience within the application. We'll create a custom registration view, form, and template.

Creating a Registration Form

1. **Define a Registration Form**:
   - o Use Django's `UserCreationForm`, which includes fields for username and password, or create a custom form to add additional fields like email.
   - o Example:

```python
Copy code
from django import forms
from django.contrib.auth.models import User
from django.contrib.auth.forms import UserCreationForm
```

```
class RegistrationForm(UserCreationForm):
    email                                   =
forms.EmailField(required=True)

    class Meta:
        model = User
        fields   =   ['username',   'email',
'password1', 'password2']
```

2. Creating the Registration View:
- Define a view in `views.py` that handles form submission, creates a new user, and redirects to the login page.
- Example:

```python
Copy code
from    django.shortcuts    import    render,
redirect
from .forms import RegistrationForm

def register(request):
    if request.method == 'POST':
        form                                    =
RegistrationForm(request.POST)
        if form.is_valid():
            form.save()
            return redirect('login')
    else:
        form = RegistrationForm()
    return                          render(request,
'register.html', {'form': form})
```

3. Rendering the Registration Template:
- Create a `register.html` template to display the form.
- Example:

```html
Copy code
<h2>Register</h2>
<form method="post">
```

```
{% csrf_token %}
{{ form.as_p }}
<button
type="submit">Register</button>
</form>
```

3. User Login and Logout

Django provides built-in views for login and logout, allowing developers to handle these functionalities quickly.

Login

1. **Using Django's Built-In LoginView**:
   o Django's `LoginView` handles the login process and requires only a template. Configure the login URL in `urls.py`.
   o Example:

   ```python
   Copy code
   from    django.contrib.auth.views    import
   LoginView

   urlpatterns = [
       path('login/',
   LoginView.as_view(template_name='login.ht
   ml'), name='login'),
   ]
   ```

2. **Creating the Login Template**:
   o Create a `login.html` template that displays Django's `AuthenticationForm`.
   o Example:

   ```html
   Copy code
   <h2>Login</h2>
   ```

```
<form method="post">
    {% csrf_token %}
    {{ form.as_p }}
    <button type="submit">Login</button>
</form>
```

3. **Redirecting After Login**:
   - Configure `LOGIN_REDIRECT_URL` in `settings.py` to control where users are redirected after login.
   - Example:

```python
Copy code
LOGIN_REDIRECT_URL = 'home'
```

Logout

1. **Using Django's LogoutView**:
   - Use Django's `LogoutView` to handle the logout process.
   - Example:

```python
Copy code
from    django.contrib.auth.views    import
LogoutView

urlpatterns = [
    path('logout/', LogoutView.as_view(),
name='logout'),
]
```

2. **Adding a Logout Link**:
   - Add a logout link in templates that redirects users to `LogoutView`.
   - Example:

```html
Copy code
<a href="{% url 'logout' %}">Logout</a>
```

4. Password Management

Password management allows users to reset their passwords if they forget them and to change passwords from within the app. Django provides built-in views and forms for handling password management securely.

Password Reset

1. **Using Django's PasswordResetView**:
   - `PasswordResetView` sends a password reset email to the user. Configure `EMAIL_BACKEND` in `settings.py` to use a real email server or Django's console backend for development.
   - Example:

   ```python
   python
   Copy code
   from django.contrib.auth.views import PasswordResetView

   urlpatterns = [
       path('password_reset/',
   PasswordResetView.as_view(),
   name='password_reset'),
   ]
   ```

2. **Configuring Email Backend**:
   - Set up `EMAIL_BACKEND` in `settings.py` to test password reset emails.
   - Example (console backend for testing):

```
python
Copy code
EMAIL_BACKEND                              =
'django.core.mail.backends.console.EmailB
ackend'
```

3. **Creating Password Reset Templates**:
   - ○ Django requires several templates for password reset (e.g., `password_reset.html`, `password_reset_done.html`). Use Django's documentation to style these templates as needed.

Password Change

1. **Using PasswordChangeView**:
   - ○ `PasswordChangeView` allows users to change their password when logged in.
   - ○ Example:

```
python
Copy code
from    django.contrib.auth.views    import
PasswordChangeView

urlpatterns = [
    path('password_change/',
PasswordChangeView.as_view(),
name='password_change'),
]
```

2. **Creating the Password Change Template**:
   - ○ Create a `password_change.html` template to display the password change form.

5. Access Control with Roles and Permissions

Roles and permissions restrict access to certain pages or actions based on user roles, enhancing security and enabling role-based functionality.

Using Django's Permissions System

1. **Default Permissions**:
   - Django assigns basic permissions (e.g., add, change, delete) to each model. These permissions can be customized for specific needs.
2. **Custom Permissions**:
   - Define custom permissions in models using Meta options.
   - Example:

```python
Copy code
class Article(models.Model):
    title                        =
models.CharField(max_length=100)

    class Meta:
        permissions = [
            ("can_publish", "Can publish
articles"),
        ]
```

Using Groups to Assign Roles

1. **Creating Groups**:
   - In the Django admin panel, create groups for each role (e.g., Admin, Moderator, User) and assign permissions to these groups.
2. **Assigning Users to Groups**:

o Assign users to specific groups, giving them access to certain views and actions based on their roles.

Restricting Access with Decorators

1. **Using @login_required:**
   o Restrict views to authenticated users by adding the @login_required decorator.
   o Example:

   ```python
   Copy code
   from django.contrib.auth.decorators import login_required

   @login_required
   def dashboard(request):
       return                 render(request,
   'dashboard.html')
   ```

2. **Using @permission_required:**
   o Restrict views to users with specific permissions using the @permission_required decorator.
   o Example:

   ```python
   Copy code
   from django.contrib.auth.decorators import permission_required

   @permission_required('app.can_publish')
   def publish_article(request):
       # Article publishing logic
   ```

3. **Using Class-Based View Mixins:**

o   `LoginRequiredMixin` **and** `PermissionRequiredMixin` can be used with CBVs to enforce access control.
o   Example:

```python
Copy code
from django.contrib.auth.mixins import
LoginRequiredMixin,
PermissionRequiredMixin
from django.views.generic import ListView
from .models import Article

class ArticleListView(LoginRequiredMixin,
PermissionRequiredMixin, ListView):
    model = Article
    permission_required =
'app.can_publish'
    template_name = 'article_list.html'
```

6. Real-World Example: User Roles and Dashboard Access Control

Let's implement a dashboard with restricted access for different user roles. For this example, we'll create a simple dashboard where admins can view a summary of users and content.

Step 1: Define Roles and Permissions

1. **Creating Groups**:
    o   In Django's admin panel, create groups (e.g., Admin and Editor). Assign permissions for managing content based on the group.
2. **Customizing User Roles**:
    o   Assign users to the Admin or Editor group depending on their responsibilities.

Step 2: Building the Dashboard View

1. **Defining a Restricted Dashboard View**:
   o Create a view restricted to Admin users.
   o Example:

```python
Copy code
from django.contrib.auth.decorators import
login_required, user_passes_test

def is_admin(user):
    return
user.groups.filter(name='Admin').exists()

@login_required
@user_passes_test(is_admin)
def admin_dashboard(request):
    return                         render(request,
'admin_dashboard.html')
```

2. **Creating the Dashboard Template**:
   o In `admin_dashboard.html`, include a summary of user registrations, recent content, or other relevant data.

Step 3: Adding Links and Navigation Based on Role

1. **Conditional Navigation**:
   o Use conditional statements in templates to display links based on the user's role.
   o Example:

```html
Copy code
{%                                          if
request.user.groups.filter(name="Admin").
exists %}
    <a    href="{%    url    'admin_dashboard'
%}">Admin Dashboard</a>
```

```
{% endif %}
```

7. Summary

In this chapter, we explored Django's built-in authentication system, covering user registration, login, logout, and password management. We implemented access control with roles and permissions, allowing different user roles to access specific parts of the application. Mastering authentication and user management is essential for building secure, user-focused applications, and Django's authentication framework provides a powerful, flexible foundation for these features.

CHAPTER 11: WORKING WITH STATIC AND MEDIA FILES

Static files (CSS, JavaScript, images) and media files (user-uploaded content) are essential for creating visually appealing, interactive, and functional web applications. Django provides tools for managing these files effectively, whether they're part of the app's assets or uploaded by users. In this chapter, we'll configure Django for static and media file management, explore best practices for organizing and serving these files, and build an image gallery as a real-world example of handling user uploads.

1. Introduction to Static and Media Files in Django

Static files refer to files like CSS, JavaScript, and images that don't change over time, whereas media files are typically user-uploaded content like profile pictures or documents. Django's `static` and `media` directories keep these file types separate for organization and performance.

Key Differences Between Static and Media Files

1. **Static Files**:
   o These files are necessary for styling (CSS), interactivity (JavaScript), and other elements that don't change based on user input. Static files are generally loaded once and cached by the browser for faster load times.
2. **Media Files**:

o Media files are user-generated content, such as uploaded images or documents. They require special handling because they are unique to each user or session and cannot be preloaded or cached like static files.

2. Configuring Static Files

Static files are usually served from a `static` folder in Django. To work with static files effectively, configure your project's settings and organize files into appropriate directories.

Setting Up Static File Configuration

1. **Configuring Static File Settings in `settings.py`**:
   o **Define** `STATIC_URL` **and** `STATICFILES_DIRS` **in** `settings.py` **to specify where Django should look for static files and what URL prefix to use when serving them.**
   o **Example:**

```python
Copy code
STATIC_URL = '/static/'
STATICFILES_DIRS = [
    BASE_DIR / 'static',
]
```

2. **Using `static` Template Tag**:
   o **Use the** `{% static %}` **template tag to reference static files in templates, ensuring they load correctly regardless of the environment.**
   o **Example:**

```html
Copy code
```

```
<link   rel="stylesheet"   href="{%   static
'css/styles.css' %}">
```

3. **Collecting Static Files for Production**:
    o Use the `collectstatic` management command to gather all static files into a single directory (`STATIC_ROOT`) before deployment.
    o Example:

    ```bash
    bash
    Copy code
    python manage.py collectstatic
    ```

    o Define `STATIC_ROOT` in `settings.py`:

    ```python
    python
    Copy code
    STATIC_ROOT = BASE_DIR / 'staticfiles'
    ```

Organizing Static Files

1. **Directory Structure**:
    o Organize files by type (e.g., `css`, `js`, `images`) or app name to keep the static directory organized.
    o Example:

    ```arduino
    arduino
    Copy code
    static/
        css/
            styles.css
        js/
            scripts.js
        images/
            logo.png
    ```

2. **Static Files in Individual Apps**:
    o Place app-specific static files in each app's `static` folder to keep them self-contained and modular.

o Example:

```arduino
Copy code
myapp/
    static/
        myapp/
            css/
            js/
            images/
```

3. Configuring Media Files

Media files are user-generated content that requires different handling from static files, as they are uploaded dynamically. In Django, media files are stored in a separate directory, defined by MEDIA_URL and MEDIA_ROOT.

Setting Up Media File Configuration

1. **Configuring Media Settings in settings.py:**
    o Define MEDIA_URL and MEDIA_ROOT to specify where media files should be stored and the URL path for accessing them.
    o Example:

    ```python
    Copy code
    MEDIA_URL = '/media/'
    MEDIA_ROOT = BASE_DIR / 'media'
    ```

2. **Serving Media Files During Development:**
    o During development, serve media files using Django's development server by adding a configuration to urls.py.
    o Example in urls.py:

```python
Copy code
from django.conf import settings
from django.conf.urls.static import static

if settings.DEBUG:
    urlpatterns                               +=
static(settings.MEDIA_URL,
document_root=settings.MEDIA_ROOT)
```

Using FileField and ImageField for Media Uploads

1. **FileField and ImageField in Models**:
   - Django provides `FileField` and `ImageField` for handling uploaded files. `ImageField` requires the Python Imaging Library (Pillow) for image processing.
   - Example:

```python
Copy code
from django.db import models

class Profile(models.Model):
    name                                      =
models.CharField(max_length=100)
    profile_picture                           =
models.ImageField(upload_to='profile_pics
/')
```

2. **Using the `upload_to` Argument**:
   - The `upload_to` argument defines the directory where uploaded files will be stored, making it easier to organize files.
   - Example:

```python
Copy code
class Document(models.Model):
    file                                      =
models.FileField(upload_to='documents/')
```

4. Handling File Uploads with Forms

Django's forms framework simplifies handling file uploads by providing `FileField` and `ImageField` form fields, allowing you to validate and process file data securely.

Creating an Upload Form

1. **Creating a Form with FileField or ImageField**:
   - Define a form for file uploads with `forms.FileField` or `forms.ImageField`.
   - Example:

   ```python
   Copy code
   from django import forms

   class UploadForm(forms.Form):
       file = forms.FileField()
   ```

2. **Enabling File Uploads in Templates**:
   - To allow file uploads in an HTML form, set `enctype="multipart/form-data"`.
   - Example:

   ```html
   Copy code
   <form                         method="post"
   enctype="multipart/form-data">
       {% csrf_token %}
       {{ form.as_p }}
       <button type="submit">Upload</button>
   </form>
   ```

3. **Handling File Uploads in Views**:
   o Handle uploaded files in views by checking `request.FILES`.
   o Example:

```python
Copy code
from django.shortcuts import render
from .forms import UploadForm

def upload_file(request):
    if request.method == 'POST':
        form = UploadForm(request.POST,
request.FILES)
        if form.is_valid():
            # Handle uploaded file
            file = request.FILES['file']
            # Save or process file
            return redirect('success')
    else:
        form = UploadForm()
    return render(request, 'upload.html',
{'form': form})
```

5. Real-World Example: Building an Image Gallery with User Uploads

Let's apply these concepts by creating an image gallery where users can upload, view, and manage images. This example will cover model creation, form handling, and displaying uploaded images in the template.

Step 1: Define the Image Model

1. **Create an `Image` Model**:
   o Define an `Image` model with fields for the image file and optional metadata.
   o Example:

```python
Copy code
from django.db import models

class Image(models.Model):
    title                    =
models.CharField(max_length=100)
    image_file               =
models.ImageField(upload_to='gallery/')
    uploaded_at              =
models.DateTimeField(auto_now_add=True)
```

Step 2: Create an Upload Form

1. **Define an Image Upload Form**:
   o **Create a** `ImageUploadForm` **with** `ImageField` **to** handle image uploads.
   o Example:

```python
Copy code
from django import forms
from .models import Image

class ImageUploadForm(forms.ModelForm):
    class Meta:
        model = Image
        fields = ['title', 'image_file']
```

Step 3: Implement Views for Upload and Display

1. **Create an Image Upload View**:
   o Define a view to handle image uploads, save the uploaded image, and redirect to the gallery.
   o Example:

```python
Copy code
from    django.shortcuts    import    render,
redirect
from .forms import ImageUploadForm
```

```
def upload_image(request):
    if request.method == 'POST':
        form                        =
ImageUploadForm(request.POST,
request.FILES)
        if form.is_valid():
            form.save()
            return redirect('gallery')
    else:
        form = ImageUploadForm()
    return                  render(request,
'upload_image.html', {'form': form})
```

2. **Create a Gallery View**:
   o Define a view to retrieve all uploaded images and pass them to the gallery template.
   o Example:

```python
Copy code
from django.shortcuts import render
from .models import Image

def gallery(request):
    images = Image.objects.all()
    return render(request, 'gallery.html',
{'images': images})
```

Step 4: Build Templates for Upload and Gallery Display

1. **Upload Template (`upload_image.html`)**:
   o Create an HTML template for the image upload form.
   o Example:

```html
Copy code
<h2>Upload Image</h2>
<form                          method="post"
enctype="multipart/form-data">
    {% csrf_token %}
```

```
{{ form.as_p }}
    <button type="submit">Upload</button>
</form>
```

2. **Gallery Template (`gallery.html`)**:
   o Design a template to display uploaded images in a grid or list format.
   o Example:

```html
Copy code
<h2>Image Gallery</h2>
<div class="gallery">
    {% for image in images %}
        <div class="image-item">
            <h3>{{ image.title }}</h3>
            <img                      src="{{
image.image_file.url          }}"          alt="{{
image.title }}">
                <p>Uploaded          on          {{
image.uploaded_at }}</p>
        </div>
    {% endfor %}
</div>
```

6. Best Practices for Managing Static and Media Files

Managing static and media files efficiently is crucial for optimizing performance and scalability in production.

Optimizing File Sizes and Formats

1. **Use Compressed Image Formats**:
   o Compress images (e.g., JPEG, PNG) before uploading to minimize file size and improve loading times.
2. **Minify CSS and JavaScript**:

- o Minify CSS and JavaScript files for faster load times. Use tools like `django-compressor` to automate this in Django.

Securing File Uploads

1. **Validate File Types**:
   - o Validate file types (e.g., restrict uploads to certain image formats) to prevent users from uploading malicious files.
2. **Restrict Access to Sensitive Files**:
   - o Store sensitive media files in private directories and set permissions carefully to avoid unauthorized access.

7. Summary

In this chapter, we explored Django's static and media file handling, covering configuration, management, and best practices. We built an image gallery with user-uploaded images as a practical example, demonstrating how to handle file uploads and display them dynamically in templates. With this understanding of static and media files, you'll be able to create visually engaging, interactive applications that integrate user content and optimized assets seamlessly.

CHAPTER 12: INTEGRATING APIS AND THIRD-PARTY SERVICES

APIs (Application Programming Interfaces) allow Django applications to interact with external systems and services, such as payment gateways, social media platforms, or data providers. By integrating APIs, you can extend your application's functionality without having to build all the features from scratch. In this chapter, we'll learn how to interact with external APIs, manage third-party integrations, and demonstrate a real-world example of fetching and displaying live data from an API.

1. Understanding APIs and How They Work

APIs are tools that enable communication between applications, allowing them to share data and perform tasks. By using APIs, Django applications can leverage functionality provided by external services.

Types of APIs

1. **REST (Representational State Transfer)**:
    - RESTful APIs use HTTP requests to retrieve and manipulate data. They are commonly used and are structured around HTTP methods like `GET`, `POST`, `PUT`, and `DELETE`.
2. **GraphQL**:
    - GraphQL is a flexible query language that allows clients to request specific data in a single

request. It's often preferred for its efficiency, especially in applications with complex data relationships.

Key API Terminology

1. **Endpoints**:
   o API endpoints are URLs through which applications interact with the API. Each endpoint serves a specific function, such as retrieving data or updating a record.
2. **Authentication**:
   o Many APIs require authentication, typically through API keys, OAuth tokens, or access tokens, to ensure secure access.
3. **Rate Limits**:
   o APIs often have rate limits to control the number of requests allowed over a certain time period. Rate limits prevent excessive usage and protect the API provider's infrastructure.

2. Working with REST APIs in Django

To work with REST APIs in Django, you'll typically use Python's `requests` library, which simplifies HTTP requests and makes it easy to interact with external APIs.

Setting Up the `requests` Library

1. **Installing `requests`**:
   o If it's not already installed, add `requests` to your project:

```bash
Copy code
```

```
pip install requests
```

2. Using `requests` for Basic API Requests:

- The `requests` library provides simple methods (`get`, `post`, `put`, `delete`) to interact with REST APIs.
- Example:

```python
Copy code
import requests

response                                    =
requests.get('https://api.example.com/dat
a')
if response.status_code == 200:
    data = response.json()   # Parse the
JSON response
```

Making API Requests in Django Views

1. Creating a View to Fetch API Data:

- Create a Django view that fetches data from an API and passes it to a template.
- Example:

```python
Copy code
from django.shortcuts import render
import requests

def weather_view(request):
    api_key = 'your_api_key'
    city = 'London'
    url                                     =
f'https://api.openweathermap.org/data/2.5
/weather?q={city}&appid={api_key}'
    response = requests.get(url)
    weather_data   =   response.json()   if
response.status_code == 200 else None
    return render(request, 'weather.html',
{'weather_data': weather_data})
```

2. **Handling Errors and Status Codes**:
    - Check the response's status code to ensure the request was successful, and handle errors gracefully.
    - Example:

```python
Copy code
if response.status_code == 200:
    data = response.json()
else:
    data = {'error': 'Unable to fetch
data'}
```

3. **Caching API Responses**:
    - Use Django's caching framework to cache API responses, especially for APIs with rate limits or data that doesn't change frequently. This reduces the number of API requests and improves performance.

3. Working with GraphQL APIs in Django

GraphQL APIs allow you to request specific data fields, making them efficient for complex queries. To work with GraphQL APIs, you can use the `requests` library or the `gql` library.

Making a GraphQL Request

1. **Setting Up a Basic GraphQL Request**:
    - Send a POST request with a query string to the GraphQL endpoint.
    - Example:

```python
Copy code
import requests
```

```
url                                          =
'https://graphql.example.com/graphql'
query = '''
{
    user(id: "1") {
        name
        email
    }
}
'''
response          =          requests.post(url,
json={'query': query})
data = response.json()
```

2. **Using Variables in GraphQL Queries**:
   o Many GraphQL APIs support variable-based queries, allowing you to define parameters dynamically.
   o Example:

```python
Copy code
query = '''
query GetUser($id: ID!) {
    user(id: $id) {
        name
        email
    }
}
'''
variables = {'id': '1'}
response         =          requests.post(url,
json={'query':     query,      'variables':
variables})
```

Using the gql Library for GraphQL

1. **Setting Up the gql Library**:
   o Install gql for more advanced GraphQL requests:

```bash
bash
```

```
Copy code
pip install gql
```

o **Example usage with** `gql`:

```python
python
Copy code
from gql import gql, Client
from     gql.transport.requests     import
RequestsHTTPTransport

transport                              =
RequestsHTTPTransport(url='https://graphq
l.example.com/graphql')
client   =   Client(transport=transport,
fetch_schema_from_transport=True)
query = gql('''
{
    user(id: "1") {
        name
        email
    }
}
''')
result = client.execute(query)
```

4. Handling API Authentication

Many APIs require authentication, which can be achieved through API keys, OAuth, or access tokens. Django's `requests` library supports adding headers to requests, which is commonly used for authentication.

Using API Key Authentication

1. **Passing API Key in the Headers**:
   o Include the API key in the headers or as a query parameter, depending on the API's requirements.

o   **Example:**

```python
Copy code
headers   =   {'Authorization':   'Bearer
your_api_key'}
response                               =
requests.get('https://api.example.com/dat
a', headers=headers)
```

Using OAuth for Secure Access

1. **OAuth Flow**:
   o   OAuth is a secure authentication method used by many APIs, including social media platforms. For Django, use libraries like `django-allauth` or `requests-oauthlib` for OAuth integration.
   o   **Example with** `requests-oauthlib`:

```bash
Copy code
pip install requests-oauthlib
```

   o   **Example OAuth code:**

```python
Copy code
from       requests_oauthlib        import
OAuth1Session

oauth    =     OAuth1Session(client_key,
client_secret,          resource_owner_key,
resource_owner_secret)
response                               =
oauth.get('https://api.example.com/protec
ted')
```

5. Integrating Third-Party Services in Django

Third-party services, such as payment gateways, email providers, and mapping APIs, extend the functionality of Django applications without requiring custom development for these complex features.

Integrating a Payment Gateway (e.g., Stripe)

1. **Setting Up Stripe in Django**:
   o Install the Stripe SDK and configure API keys.
   o Example:

   ```bash
   bash
   Copy code
   pip install stripe
   ```

2. **Creating a Payment View**:
   o Use Stripe's API to create a payment session, then render the session details in a template.
   o Example:

   ```python
   python
   Copy code
   import stripe
   from django.conf import settings
   from django.shortcuts import render

   stripe.api_key                        =
   settings.STRIPE_SECRET_KEY

   def create_checkout_session(request):
       session                           =
   stripe.checkout.Session.create(
           payment_method_types=['card'],
           line_items=[{
               'price_data': {
                   'currency': 'usd',
                   'product_data': {
                       'name':          'Sample
   Product',
                   },
                   'unit_amount': 1000,
   ```

```
            },
            'quantity': 1,
        }],
        mode='payment',

    success_url='https://yourdomain.com/succe
    ss',

    cancel_url='https://yourdomain.com/cancel
    ',
        )
        return            render(request,
    'checkout.html',        {'session_id':
    session.id})
```

Using an Email Provider API (e.g., SendGrid)

1. **Setting Up SendGrid in Django**:
   o Install the SendGrid library and configure API keys.
   o Example:

   ```bash
   Copy code
   pip install sendgrid
   ```

2. **Creating a Function to Send Emails**:
   o Use SendGrid's API to send transactional emails directly from Django.
   o Example:

   ```python
   Copy code
   from sendgrid import SendGridAPIClient
   from sendgrid.helpers.mail import Mail
   from django.conf import settings

   def     send_email(to_email,      subject,
   content):
       message = Mail(

   from_email=settings.SENDGRID_FROM_EMAIL,
   ```

```
              to_emails=to_email,
              subject=subject,
              html_content=content)
        try:
              sg                        =
SendGridAPIClient(settings.SENDGRID_API_K
EY)
              response = sg.send(message)
        except Exception as e:
              print(e)
```

6. Real-World Example: Fetching and Displaying Live Data from an API

Let's create a feature to fetch live weather data from an external API and display it in a Django template.

Step 1: Set Up the API Request

1. **Define the API Endpoint**:
   o Use a weather API, such as OpenWeatherMap, to get current weather data based on the city.
   o Example:

```python
Copy code
import requests
from django.conf import settings

def get_weather(city):
    api_key = settings.OPENWEATHER_API_KEY
    url                                  =
f'http://api.openweathermap.org/data/2.5/
weather?q={city}&appid={api_key}'
    response = requests.get(url)
    return        response.json()        if
response.status_code == 200 else None
```

Step 2: Create a View to Fetch Weather Data

1. **Define the Weather View**:
   o Use the API function in a view and pass the data to a template.
   o Example:

```python
Copy code
from django.shortcuts import render

def weather_view(request):
    city      =      request.GET.get('city',
'London')
    weather_data = get_weather(city)
    return render(request, 'weather.html',
{'weather_data': weather_data})
```

Step 3: Build the Template for Display

1. **Create the Weather Display Template**:
   o In `weather.html`, display the weather data in a structured format.
   o Example:

```html
Copy code
<h2>Weather    for    {{    weather_data.name
}}</h2>
<p>Temperature: {{ weather_data.main.temp
}}K</p>
<p>Weather:                              {{
weather_data.weather.0.description }}</p>
```

7. Summary

In this chapter, we explored how to use Django to integrate APIs and third-party services, covering both REST and GraphQL APIs. We demonstrated techniques for handling API authentication, managing third-party services like Stripe and SendGrid, and provided a practical example of fetching live data from an external API. With this knowledge, you can extend your Django application to integrate powerful external services and provide dynamic, data-driven functionality to your users.

CHAPTER 13:HANDLING ASYNCHRONOUS TASKS WITH CELERY

In a web application, certain tasks, like sending emails or processing data, can take time and slow down the response to the user. To handle these long-running tasks asynchronously, we can use Celery, a distributed task queue system. Celery integrates seamlessly with Django, allowing you to run tasks in the background without impacting the user experience. In this chapter, we'll explore setting up Celery with Django, learn to configure it for different types of tasks, and build a real-world example of sending automated email notifications.

1. Introduction to Asynchronous Tasks

Asynchronous tasks enable web applications to offload time-consuming processes, making them ideal for tasks that don't require an immediate response to the user.

Why Use Asynchronous Tasks?

1. **Improving User Experience**:
   o Offloading tasks to the background prevents blocking the main application, leading to faster response times and a smoother user experience.
2. **Managing High-Volume Tasks**:

- By distributing tasks across workers, asynchronous task queues can handle multiple tasks simultaneously, making them well-suited for high-traffic applications.

3. **Examples of Asynchronous Tasks**:
   - Examples include sending emails, generating reports, processing large files, and integrating third-party services.

2. Setting Up Celery with Django

Celery is a powerful asynchronous task queue that can handle distributed workloads. To use Celery with Django, you'll need to install Celery and a message broker (usually Redis or RabbitMQ).

Installing Celery and Redis

1. **Installing Celery and Redis**:
   - Use pip to install Celery and Redis (or RabbitMQ) as your message broker.
   - Example:

   ```bash
   pip install celery redis
   ```

2. **Setting Up Redis as a Message Broker**:
   - Start the Redis server to enable Celery to communicate with it.
   - For most systems, you can start Redis with:

   ```bash
   Copy code
   redis-server
   ```

Configuring Celery in Django

1. **Creating a `celery.py` File**:
   - In your project directory (next to `settings.py`), create a `celery.py` file to configure Celery with Django settings.
   - Example (`myproject/celery.py`):

   ```python
   Copy code
   from __future__ import absolute_import,
   unicode_literals
   import os
   from celery import Celery

   os.environ.setdefault('DJANGO_SETTINGS_MO
   DULE', 'myproject.settings')
   app = Celery('myproject')
   app.config_from_object('django.conf:setti
   ngs', namespace='CELERY')
   app.autodiscover_tasks()
   ```

2. **Defining Celery Settings in `settings.py`**:
   - Add Celery configuration in `settings.py`, pointing to Redis as the broker.
   - Example:

   ```python
   Copy code
   CELERY_BROKER_URL                        =
   'redis://localhost:6379/0'
   CELERY_RESULT_BACKEND                    =
   'redis://localhost:6379/0'
   ```

3. **Initializing Celery in Django**:
   - In `__init__.py` of your project directory, import Celery to ensure it loads with Django.
   - Example (`myproject/__init__.py`):

   ```python
   Copy code
   from .celery import app as celery_app
   ```

```
__all__ = ('celery_app',)
```

3. Creating and Running Celery Tasks

Celery tasks are Python functions that run asynchronously. With Celery, you can decorate functions to turn them into background tasks and set task parameters like schedules and retries.

Defining a Celery Task

1. **Creating a Task**:
   - In any Django app, define a task function and decorate it with `@app.task`.
   - Example:

```python
Copy code
from celery import shared_task

@shared_task
def send_welcome_email(user_id):
    # Import here to avoid circular imports
    from django.core.mail import send_mail
    from django.contrib.auth.models import User

    user = User.objects.get(id=user_id)
    send_mail(
        'Welcome!',
        'Thanks     for     joining     us,
{}'.format(user.username),
        'from@example.com',
        [user.email],
    )
```

2. **Calling a Task in Django**:
   - Call the task function using the `.delay()` method, which queues it for execution.

o **Example:**

```python
Copy code
# In a view, call the task to send a welcome
email after user registration
send_welcome_email.delay(user.id)
```

3. **Running the Celery Worker**:
   o Start a Celery worker to listen for tasks.
   o Example command:

```bash
Copy code
celery -A myproject worker --loglevel=info
```

Task Options

1. **Retrying Failed Tasks**:
   o Use the `retry` parameter to re-attempt a task if it fails.
   o Example:

```python
Copy code
@shared_task(bind=True, max_retries=3)
def task_with_retry(self):
    try:
        # Some code that might fail
        pass
    except Exception as exc:
        raise self.retry(exc=exc)
```

2. **Setting Task Time Limits**:
   o Set a `time_limit` to stop tasks that exceed a specific runtime.
   o Example:

```python
Copy code
```

```
@shared_task(time_limit=300)
def long_running_task():
    # Task code
    pass
```

4. Scheduling Periodic Tasks

Celery can schedule tasks to run at specific intervals using Celery Beat, a scheduler that works with Celery to trigger tasks periodically.

Setting Up Celery Beat

1. **Installing Celery Beat**:
   - Install Celery Beat to manage scheduled tasks.
   - Example:

```bash
Copy code
pip install django-celery-beat
```

2. **Configuring Celery Beat**:
   - Add `django_celery_beat` to your `INSTALLED_APPS` and run migrations to set up the necessary tables.
   - Example:

```python
Copy code
INSTALLED_APPS = [
    # Other apps...
    'django_celery_beat',
]
```

3. **Starting the Beat Scheduler**:
   - Start the scheduler to activate periodic tasks.
   - Example command:

```
bash
Copy code
celery -A myproject beat --loglevel=info
```

Creating Periodic Tasks with Celery Beat

1. **Using the Django Admin Panel to Schedule Tasks**:
   o Access the Django admin interface to create periodic tasks for any registered Celery task. Configure frequency, start time, and end time directly from the admin panel.
2. **Scheduling Tasks Programmatically**:
   o You can also create periodic tasks programmatically using the `PeriodicTask` model.
   o Example:

```python
python
Copy code
from django_celery_beat.models import PeriodicTask, IntervalSchedule
from datetime import timedelta

schedule, created = IntervalSchedule.objects.get_or_create(
    every=1,
    period=IntervalSchedule.DAYS,
)

PeriodicTask.objects.create(
    interval=schedule,
    name='Daily summary email',

    task='myapp.tasks.send_daily_summary',
)
```

5. Real-World Example: Sending Automated Email Notifications

In this example, we'll use Celery to send automated email notifications to users. We'll create a task that sends a daily summary email, set it up to run periodically with Celery Beat, and configure it to retry in case of failure.

Step 1: Define the Task to Send Emails

1. **Creating the Email Task**:
   - Define a Celery task to send an email to users.
   - Example:

```python
Copy code
from celery import shared_task
from django.core.mail import send_mail
from django.utils import timezone
from datetime import timedelta
from .models import UserActivity

@shared_task
def send_daily_summary():
    yesterday = timezone.now() - timedelta(days=1)
    activities = UserActivity.objects.filter(timestamp__gte=yesterday)

    for user in User.objects.filter(is_active=True):
        user_activities = activities.filter(user=user)
        if user_activities.exists():
            send_mail(
                'Daily Summary',
                'Here is your activity summary...',
                'from@example.com',
                [user.email],
            )
```

Step 2: Schedule the Task with Celery Beat

1. **Creating a Periodic Task in the Admin Panel**:
   - Go to the Django admin, create an interval for 1 day, and set up a periodic task linked to `send_daily_summary`.
2. **Configuring Retry Logic**:
   - In the task definition, add a `retry` block in case the email fails to send.
   - Example:

```python
Copy code
@shared_task(bind=True, max_retries=3)
def send_daily_summary(self):
    try:
        # Task code here
        pass
    except Exception as exc:
        raise self.retry(exc=exc)
```

Step 3: Testing the Automated Email Task

1. **Testing the Task Locally**:
   - Manually call `send_daily_summary.delay()` from the Django shell to verify that emails are sent and that any retry logic works as expected.
2. **Monitoring Task Execution**:
   - Monitor task logs for any errors or issues, and confirm that emails are sent according to the schedule.

6. Best Practices for Celery Tasks

Using Celery effectively involves adhering to some best practices that help you maintain performance, reliability, and scalability in a production environment.

Task Optimization and Monitoring

1. **Optimize Task Granularity**:
   o Break down large tasks into smaller, independent tasks to improve efficiency and reduce memory usage.
2. **Monitor Task Failures**:
   o Use tools like Flower or Celery's monitoring commands to track task status and retry failed tasks as needed.
3. **Use Dedicated Workers for High-Priority Tasks**:
   o Assign specific workers to high-priority tasks, ensuring that important tasks get processed without delay.

7. Summary

In this chapter, we explored using Celery to handle asynchronous tasks in Django, including setup, configuration, and creating tasks that run in the background. We learned how to use Celery Beat for scheduling periodic tasks and applied these concepts in a real-world example of sending automated email notifications. By integrating Celery into your Django applications, you can enhance performance, improve user experience, and scale task processing for high-demand applications.

CHAPTER 14: BUILDING REST APIS WITH DJANGO REST FRAMEWORK

REST APIs (Representational State Transfer APIs) allow applications to communicate with each other over the web. Django REST Framework (DRF) is a powerful library for building RESTful APIs with Django, providing a robust toolkit for handling HTTP requests, data serialization, and permissions. In this chapter, we'll explore how to use DRF to create and manage REST APIs, learn about serializers and viewsets, and build a CRUD API for a sample mobile app backend.

1. Introduction to Django REST Framework (DRF)

Django REST Framework (DRF) extends Django's capabilities to create RESTful APIs efficiently, with features that simplify serialization, view handling, authentication, and permissions. DRF is well-suited for building APIs that can serve web and mobile applications.

Why Use Django REST Framework?

1. **Ease of Serialization**:
     o DRF simplifies converting data between JSON and Django model instances, making it easy to work with data in a format that web and mobile applications use.
2. **Flexible View Handling**:

- o DRF provides view classes that streamline CRUD operations (Create, Read, Update, Delete) with minimal code, ideal for building data-driven APIs.

3. **Built-in Authentication and Permissions**:
   - o DRF includes authentication and permissions out-of-the-box, helping you control access to your API endpoints.

2. Setting Up Django REST Framework

To begin building APIs, you'll need to install and configure Django REST Framework in your project.

Installing DRF

1. **Install Django REST Framework**:
   - o Use pip to install DRF:

```bash
Copy code
pip install djangorestframework
```

2. **Add DRF to INSTALLED_APPS**:
   - o In settings.py, add rest_framework to the INSTALLED_APPS list:

```python
Copy code
INSTALLED_APPS = [
    # Other apps...
    'rest_framework',
]
```

Configuring DRF

1. **Basic Configuration in settings.py**:

- o Define any custom settings for DRF, such as pagination or default permissions.
- o Example:

```python
Copy code
REST_FRAMEWORK = {
    'DEFAULT_PERMISSION_CLASSES': [

    'rest_framework.permissions.AllowAny',
        ],
        'DEFAULT_AUTHENTICATION_CLASSES': [

    'rest_framework.authentication.SessionAut
hentication',

    'rest_framework.authentication.BasicAuthe
ntication',
        ],
}
```

3. Understanding Serializers in DRF

Serializers in DRF convert complex data types (like Django models) into JSON, making data easily accessible to external applications. They also handle data validation when creating or updating model instances.

Creating a Simple Serializer

1. **Defining a Serializer for a Model**:
   - o Use `serializers.ModelSerializer` to define a serializer based on a model.
   - o Example:

```python
Copy code
from rest_framework import serializers
from .models import Product
```

```
class
ProductSerializer(serializers.ModelSerial
izer):
    class Meta:
        model = Product
        fields    =    ['id',    'name',
'description', 'price']
```

2. Customizing Serializer Fields:

- o Define extra fields or validation rules within the serializer class.
- o Example:

```python
Copy code
class
ProductSerializer(serializers.ModelSerial
izer):
    price_with_tax                    =
serializers.SerializerMethodField()

    class Meta:
        model = Product
        fields    =    ['id',    'name',
'description', 'price', 'price_with_tax']

    def get_price_with_tax(self, obj):
        return obj.price * 1.2  # Example
tax calculation
```

Using serializers.Serializer for Non-Model Data

1. Creating a Serializer for Custom Data:

- o Use serializers.Serializer when working with non-model data or when custom processing is required.
- o Example:

```python
Copy code
```

```
class
CustomSerializer(serializers.Serializer):
    name                                =
serializers.CharField(max_length=100)
    age = serializers.IntegerField()
```

4. Creating API Views with DRF

DRF provides various views for building REST APIs, including
APIView, GenericAPIView, and viewsets. These views handle
HTTP requests and integrate with serializers for data handling.

Function-Based Views with DRF

1. **Creating a Basic API View**:
   o Use DRF's @api_view decorator for quick setup
     of function-based views.
   o Example:

```python
Copy code
from    rest_framework.decorators    import
api_view
from    rest_framework.response    import
Response

@api_view(['GET'])
def hello_world(request):
    return  Response({"message":   "Hello,
World!"})
```

Class-Based Views with APIView

1. **Creating a Class-Based API View**:
   o Use APIView to handle multiple HTTP methods
     within a single class.
   o Example:

```python
Copy code
from rest_framework.views import APIView
from rest_framework.response import Response
from .models import Product
from .serializers import ProductSerializer

class ProductList(APIView):
    def get(self, request):
        products = Product.objects.all()
        serializer = ProductSerializer(products, many=True)
        return Response(serializer.data)

    def post(self, request):
        serializer = ProductSerializer(data=request.data)
        if serializer.is_valid():
            serializer.save()
            return Response(serializer.data, status=201)
        return Response(serializer.errors, status=400)
```

5. Using DRF's Generic Views and Mixins for CRUD Operations

DRF's generic views and mixins simplify common API patterns like listing objects, creating new instances, or retrieving details.

Using Generic Views

1. **`ListCreateAPIView` for List and Create**:
   o `ListCreateAPIView` provides list and create functionality for a model with minimal code.
   o Example:

   ```python
   Copy code
   ```

```
from      rest_framework.generics      import
ListCreateAPIView
from .models import Product
from .serializers import ProductSerializer

class
ProductListCreateView(ListCreateAPIView):
    queryset = Product.objects.all()
    serializer_class = ProductSerializer
```

2. **`RetrieveUpdateDestroyAPIView` for Retrieve, Update, and Delete**:
   - `RetrieveUpdateDestroyAPIView` **combines** retrieve, update, and delete functionality.
   - Example:

```python
Copy code
from      rest_framework.generics      import
RetrieveUpdateDestroyAPIView

class
ProductDetailView(RetrieveUpdateDestroyAP
IView):
    queryset = Product.objects.all()
    serializer_class = ProductSerializer
```

Using Mixins for More Control

1. **Combining Mixins with `GenericAPIView`**:
   - Mixins allow you to combine only the desired functionality, offering more control.
   - Example:

```python
Copy code
from rest_framework import mixins
from      rest_framework.generics      import
GenericAPIView
```

```
class
ProductListView(mixins.ListModelMixin,
mixins.CreateModelMixin, GenericAPIView):
    queryset = Product.objects.all()
    serializer_class = ProductSerializer

    def    get(self,    request,    *args,
**kwargs):
        return  self.list(request,  *args,
**kwargs)

    def    post(self,    request,    *args,
**kwargs):
        return self.create(request, *args,
**kwargs)
```

6. Building API Viewsets for Efficient Routing

Viewsets in DRF combine multiple views for a model into a single class, allowing for a more concise and organized API. They are often paired with routers for automatic URL generation.

Defining a Viewset

1. **Creating a Model Viewset**:
   o **Use** `ModelViewSet` **to handle full CRUD operations.**
   o **Example:**

```python
Copy code
from rest_framework import viewsets
from .models import Product
from .serializers import ProductSerializer

class
ProductViewSet(viewsets.ModelViewSet):
    queryset = Product.objects.all()
    serializer_class = ProductSerializer
```

Using Routers with Viewsets

1. **Defining a Router in** `urls.py`:
   - ○ DRF's routers automatically generate URL patterns for viewsets, simplifying routing.
   - ○ Example in `urls.py`:

```python
Copy code
from     rest_framework.routers    import
DefaultRouter
from .views import ProductViewSet

router = DefaultRouter()
router.register(r'products',
ProductViewSet)

urlpatterns = router.urls
```

7. Adding Authentication and Permissions

DRF includes built-in authentication classes (e.g., session, token) and permissions to secure your API. Permissions control who can access which views and what actions they can perform.

Adding Authentication

1. **Setting Up Token Authentication**:
   - ○ Install `djangorestframework-simplejwt` **for** JWT-based token authentication.
   - ○ Example setup:

```bash
Copy code
pip install djangorestframework-simplejwt
```

2. **Configuring Authentication in** `settings.py`:

o **Example:**

```python
Copy code
REST_FRAMEWORK = {
    'DEFAULT_AUTHENTICATION_CLASSES': [

'rest_framework_simplejwt.authentication.
JWTAuthentication',
    ],
}
```

Applying Permissions to Views

1. **Using DRF Permissions**:
   o Apply `IsAuthenticated` or custom permissions to control access to views.
   o **Example:**

```python
Copy code
from   rest_framework.permissions   import
IsAuthenticated

class
ProductViewSet(viewsets.ModelViewSet):
    permission_classes = [IsAuthenticated]
    queryset = Product.objects.all()
    serializer_class = ProductSerializer
```

2. **Creating Custom Permissions**:
   o Define custom permissions by inheriting from `BasePermission`.
   o **Example:**

```python
Copy code
from   rest_framework.permissions   import
BasePermission

class IsAdminUser(BasePermission):
```

```
def    has_permission(self,    request,
view):
        return        request.user        and
request.user.is_staff
```

8. Real-World Example: Building a CRUD API for a Mobile App Backend

Let's create an API for managing a simple product catalog, where users can view, add, edit, and delete products.

Step 1: Define the Product Model

1. **Create a Product Model**:
   o Define fields for a simple product catalog.
   o Example:

```python
Copy code
from django.db import models

class Product(models.Model):
    name                              =
models.CharField(max_length=100)
    description = models.TextField()
    price                             =
models.DecimalField(max_digits=10,
decimal_places=2)
    stock = models.IntegerField()
```

Step 2: Create the Serializer

1. **Define a Serializer for Product**:
   o Create a `ProductSerializer` for the model.
   o Example:

```python
```

```
Copy code
from rest_framework import serializers
from .models import Product

class
ProductSerializer(serializers.ModelSerial
izer):
    class Meta:
        model = Product
        fields    =        ['id',      'name',
'description', 'price', 'stock']
```

Step 3: Implement the Viewset

1. **Define a Viewset for Product CRUD**:
   o Use a viewset to handle all CRUD operations.
   o Example:

```python
Copy code
from rest_framework import viewsets
from .models import Product
from .serializers import ProductSerializer

class
ProductViewSet(viewsets.ModelViewSet):
    queryset = Product.objects.all()
    serializer_class = ProductSerializer
```

Step 4: Set Up Routing

1. **Use a Router to Define URLs**:
   o Register the viewset with a router in `urls.py`.
   o Example:

```python
Copy code
from     rest_framework.routers     import
DefaultRouter
from .views import ProductViewSet

router = DefaultRouter()
```

```
router.register(r'products',
ProductViewSet)

urlpatterns = router.urls
```

9. Summary

In this chapter, we explored Django REST Framework (DRF) for building REST APIs, covering essential concepts like serializers, views, viewsets, and routers. We also implemented authentication and permissions and created a CRUD API for a sample product catalog to demonstrate DRF's capabilities. By mastering DRF, you can build robust and flexible APIs for web and mobile applications, making your Django application a powerful backend solution for modern projects.

CHAPTER 14: BUILDING REST APIS WITH DJANGO REST FRAMEWORK

REST APIs (Representational State Transfer APIs) allow applications to communicate with each other over the web. Django REST Framework (DRF) is a powerful library for building RESTful APIs with Django, providing a robust toolkit for handling HTTP requests, data serialization, and permissions. In this chapter, we'll explore how to use DRF to create and manage REST APIs, learn about serializers and viewsets, and build a CRUD API for a sample mobile app backend.

1. Introduction to Django REST Framework (DRF)

Django REST Framework (DRF) extends Django's capabilities to create RESTful APIs efficiently, with features that simplify serialization, view handling, authentication, and permissions. DRF is well-suited for building APIs that can serve web and mobile applications.

Why Use Django REST Framework?

1. **Ease of Serialization**:
    o DRF simplifies converting data between JSON and Django model instances, making it easy to

work with data in a format that web and mobile applications use.

2. **Flexible View Handling**:
   - DRF provides view classes that streamline CRUD operations (Create, Read, Update, Delete) with minimal code, ideal for building data-driven APIs.

3. **Built-in Authentication and Permissions**:
   - DRF includes authentication and permissions out-of-the-box, helping you control access to your API endpoints.

2. Setting Up Django REST Framework

To begin building APIs, you'll need to install and configure Django REST Framework in your project.

Installing DRF

1. **Install Django REST Framework**:
   - Use pip to install DRF:

```bash
Copy code
pip install djangorestframework
```

2. **Add DRF to INSTALLED_APPS**:
   - In settings.py, add rest_framework to the INSTALLED_APPS list:

```python
Copy code
INSTALLED_APPS = [
    # Other apps...
    'rest_framework',
]
```

Configuring DRF

1. **Basic Configuration in** `settings.py`:
   - Define any custom settings for DRF, such as pagination or default permissions.
   - Example:

```python
Copy code
REST_FRAMEWORK = {
    'DEFAULT_PERMISSION_CLASSES': [

'rest_framework.permissions.AllowAny',
    ],
    'DEFAULT_AUTHENTICATION_CLASSES': [

'rest_framework.authentication.SessionAut
hentication',

'rest_framework.authentication.BasicAuthe
ntication',
    ],
}
```

3. Understanding Serializers in DRF

Serializers in DRF convert complex data types (like Django models) into JSON, making data easily accessible to external applications. They also handle data validation when creating or updating model instances.

Creating a Simple Serializer

1. **Defining a Serializer for a Model**:
   - Use `serializers.ModelSerializer` to define a serializer based on a model.
   - Example:

```python
```

```
Copy code
from rest_framework import serializers
from .models import Product

class
ProductSerializer(serializers.ModelSerial
izer):
    class Meta:
        model = Product
        fields      =      ['id',      'name',
'description', 'price']
```

2. Customizing Serializer Fields:

- o Define extra fields or validation rules within the serializer class.
- o Example:

```python
Copy code
class
ProductSerializer(serializers.ModelSerial
izer):
    price_with_tax                        =
serializers.SerializerMethodField()

    class Meta:
        model = Product
        fields      =      ['id',      'name',
'description', 'price', 'price_with_tax']

    def get_price_with_tax(self, obj):
        return obj.price * 1.2  # Example
tax calculation
```

Using `serializers.Serializer` *for Non-Model Data*

1. Creating a Serializer for Custom Data:

- o Use `serializers.Serializer` when working with non-model data or when custom processing is required.
- o Example:

```python
Copy code
class
CustomSerializer(serializers.Serializer):
    name                                    =
serializers.CharField(max_length=100)
    age = serializers.IntegerField()
```

4. Creating API Views with DRF

DRF provides various views for building REST APIs, including `APIView`, `GenericAPIView`, and viewsets. These views handle HTTP requests and integrate with serializers for data handling.

Function-Based Views with DRF

1. **Creating a Basic API View**:
   o Use DRF's `@api_view` decorator for quick setup of function-based views.
   o Example:

```python
Copy code
from    rest_framework.decorators    import
api_view
from    rest_framework.response    import
Response

@api_view(['GET'])
def hello_world(request):
    return    Response({"message":    "Hello,
World!"})
```

Class-Based Views with `APIView`

1. **Creating a Class-Based API View**:

- o Use `APIView` to handle multiple HTTP methods within a single class.
- o Example:

```python
Copy code
from rest_framework.views import APIView
from    rest_framework.response    import
Response
from .models import Product
from .serializers import ProductSerializer

class ProductList(APIView):
    def get(self, request):
        products = Product.objects.all()
        serializer                     =
ProductSerializer(products, many=True)
        return Response(serializer.data)

    def post(self, request):
        serializer                     =
ProductSerializer(data=request.data)
        if serializer.is_valid():
            serializer.save()
            return
Response(serializer.data, status=201)
        return Response(serializer.errors,
status=400)
```

5. Using DRF's Generic Views and Mixins for CRUD Operations

DRF's generic views and mixins simplify common API patterns like listing objects, creating new instances, or retrieving details.

Using Generic Views

1. **`ListCreateAPIView` for List and Create**:
   - o `ListCreateAPIView` provides list and create functionality for a model with minimal code.

o **Example:**

```python
Copy code
from     rest_framework.generics     import
ListCreateAPIView
from .models import Product
from .serializers import ProductSerializer

class
ProductListCreateView(ListCreateAPIView):
    queryset = Product.objects.all()
    serializer_class = ProductSerializer
```

2. **`RetrieveUpdateDestroyAPIView` for Retrieve, Update, and Delete**:
   o RetrieveUpdateDestroyAPIView   **combines** retrieve, update, and delete functionality.
   o **Example:**

```python
Copy code
from     rest_framework.generics     import
RetrieveUpdateDestroyAPIView

class
ProductDetailView(RetrieveUpdateDestroyAP
IView):
    queryset = Product.objects.all()
    serializer_class = ProductSerializer
```

Using Mixins for More Control

1. **Combining Mixins with `GenericAPIView`:**
   o Mixins allow you to combine only the desired functionality, offering more control.
   o **Example:**

```python
Copy code
from rest_framework import mixins
```

```
from      rest_framework.generics      import
GenericAPIView

class
ProductListView(mixins.ListModelMixin,
mixins.CreateModelMixin, GenericAPIView):
    queryset = Product.objects.all()
    serializer_class = ProductSerializer

    def    get(self,    request,    *args,
**kwargs):
        return  self.list(request,  *args,
**kwargs)

    def    post(self,    request,    *args,
**kwargs):
        return self.create(request, *args,
**kwargs)
```

6. Building API Viewsets for Efficient Routing

Viewsets in DRF combine multiple views for a model into a single class, allowing for a more concise and organized API. They are often paired with routers for automatic URL generation.

Defining a Viewset

1. **Creating a Model Viewset**:
   o **Use** `ModelViewSet` **to handle full CRUD operations.**
   o **Example:**

   ```python
   Copy code
   from rest_framework import viewsets
   from .models import Product
   from .serializers import ProductSerializer

   class
   ProductViewSet(viewsets.ModelViewSet):
   ```

183

```
queryset = Product.objects.all()
serializer_class = ProductSerializer
```

Using Routers with Viewsets

1. **Defining a Router in `urls.py`:**
   - DRF's routers automatically generate URL patterns for viewsets, simplifying routing.
   - **Example in** `urls.py`:

   ```python
   Copy code
   from    rest_framework.routers    import
   DefaultRouter
   from .views import ProductViewSet

   router = DefaultRouter()
   router.register(r'products',
   ProductViewSet)

   urlpatterns = router.urls
   ```

7. Adding Authentication and Permissions

DRF includes built-in authentication classes (e.g., session, token) and permissions to secure your API. Permissions control who can access which views and what actions they can perform.

Adding Authentication

1. **Setting Up Token Authentication:**
   - **Install** `djangorestframework-simplejwt` **for** JWT-based token authentication.
   - **Example setup:**

   ```bash
   Copy code
   ```

```
pip install djangorestframework-simplejwt
```

2. Configuring Authentication in `settings.py`:
- Example:

```python
Copy code
REST_FRAMEWORK = {
    'DEFAULT_AUTHENTICATION_CLASSES': [

    'rest_framework_simplejwt.authentication.
    JWTAuthentication',
        ],
    }
```

Applying Permissions to Views

1. Using DRF Permissions:
- Apply `IsAuthenticated` or custom permissions to control access to views.
- Example:

```python
Copy code
from    rest_framework.permissions    import
IsAuthenticated

class
ProductViewSet(viewsets.ModelViewSet):
    permission_classes = [IsAuthenticated]
    queryset = Product.objects.all()
    serializer_class = ProductSerializer
```

2. Creating Custom Permissions:
- Define custom permissions by inheriting from `BasePermission`.
- Example:

```python
Copy code
```

```
from    rest_framework.permissions    import
BasePermission

class IsAdminUser(BasePermission):
    def    has_permission(self,    request,
view):
        return        request.user        and
request.user.is_staff
```

8. Real-World Example: Building a CRUD API for a Mobile App Backend

Let's create an API for managing a simple product catalog, where users can view, add, edit, and delete products.

Step 1: Define the Product Model

1. **Create a Product Model**:
   - Define fields for a simple product catalog.
   - Example:

```python
Copy code
from django.db import models

class Product(models.Model):
    name                                    =
models.CharField(max_length=100)
    description = models.TextField()
    price                                   =
models.DecimalField(max_digits=10,
decimal_places=2)
    stock = models.IntegerField()
```

Step 2: Create the Serializer

1. **Define a Serializer for Product**:
   - Create a ProductSerializer for the model.

- Example:

```python
Copy code
from rest_framework import serializers
from .models import Product

class
ProductSerializer(serializers.ModelSerial
izer):
    class Meta:
        model = Product
        fields    =    ['id',    'name',
'description', 'price', 'stock']
```

Step 3: Implement the Viewset

1. **Define a Viewset for Product CRUD**:
   - Use a viewset to handle all CRUD operations.
   - Example:

```python
Copy code
from rest_framework import viewsets
from .models import Product
from .serializers import ProductSerializer

class
ProductViewSet(viewsets.ModelViewSet):
    queryset = Product.objects.all()
    serializer_class = ProductSerializer
```

Step 4: Set Up Routing

1. **Use a Router to Define URLs**:
   - Register the viewset with a router in `urls.py`.
   - Example:

```python
Copy code
```

```
from      rest_framework.routers      import
DefaultRouter
from .views import ProductViewSet

router = DefaultRouter()
router.register(r'products',
ProductViewSet)

urlpatterns = router.urls
```

9. Summary

In this chapter, we explored Django REST Framework (DRF) for building REST APIs, covering essential concepts like serializers, views, viewsets, and routers. We also implemented authentication and permissions and created a CRUD API for a sample product catalog to demonstrate DRF's capabilities. By mastering DRF, you can build robust and flexible APIs for web and mobile applications, making your Django application a powerful backend solution for modern projects.

CHAPTER 16: OPTIMIZING DJANGO PERFORMANCE

Performance optimization is essential for scaling Django applications, especially as traffic grows. Django provides several tools and techniques to improve application speed and reduce load on the server. In this chapter, we'll explore how to optimize database queries, use caching effectively, and optimize template rendering for a faster, more efficient Django application.

1. Introduction to Performance Optimization

Optimizing the performance of a Django application can help reduce server costs, improve load times, and enhance user experience. Key areas to focus on include database query efficiency, caching, and template rendering.

Why Performance Optimization Matters

1. **Improving User Experience**:
   o Faster load times result in a smoother user experience and higher user retention.
2. **Reducing Server Load**:
   o Efficient applications require less server power, reducing operational costs.
3. **Handling Increased Traffic**:
   o Optimizations help applications scale smoothly when handling more users or heavier workloads.

2. Optimizing Database Queries

Database queries are one of the most performance-sensitive parts of a Django application, as inefficient queries can slow down response times. Django provides several tools to optimize query performance.

Using QuerySets Efficiently

1. **Using `select_related` and `prefetch_related`:**
   - These methods reduce the number of queries by fetching related objects in advance.
   - Example:

     ```python
     Copy code
     # Using select_related for ForeignKey
     relationships
     products                              =
     Product.objects.select_related('category'
     ).all()

     # Using prefetch_related for ManyToMany
     relationships
     orders                                =
     Order.objects.prefetch_related('items').a
     ll()
     ```

2. **Avoiding N+1 Query Problem:**
   - The N+1 problem occurs when a query fetches a related model within a loop, causing additional queries. Use `select_related` or `prefetch_related` to load data in a single query.

3. **Limiting Data with `only()` and `defer()`:**
   - `only()` and `defer()` load only specific fields, reducing data retrieval and memory usage.
   - Example:

     ```python
     ```

```
Copy code
products   =   Product.objects.only('name',
'price')
```

Reducing Database Load

1. **Using Caching for Frequently Accessed Data**:
   o Cache results of frequently accessed queries to avoid repeated database hits.
2. **Indexing Database Fields**:
   o Adding indexes to frequently queried fields can speed up lookups. Django's `Meta` class allows you to define indexes.
   o Example:

```python
Copy code
class Product(models.Model):
    name                              =
models.CharField(max_length=100)
    price                             =
models.DecimalField(max_digits=10,
decimal_places=2)

    class Meta:
        indexes = [

models.Index(fields=['name']),
        ]
```

3. **Batching Updates**:
   o Use `update()` to update multiple records at once, reducing the number of individual save calls.
   o Example:

```python
Copy code
Product.objects.filter(is_featured=True).
update(price=50)
```

3. Using Caching for Faster Load Times

Caching stores the results of expensive operations, allowing subsequent requests to load data from memory rather than re-running queries or computations. Django's caching framework makes it easy to implement caching at various levels.

Types of Caching in Django

1. **Database Query Caching**:
   - Cache results of frequent database queries to reduce database load.
2. **Template Fragment Caching**:
   - Cache parts of a template that take longer to render, such as a user dashboard or navigation bar.
   - Example:

   ```html
   Copy code
   {% load cache %}
   {% cache 600 sidebar %}
       <!-- Cached content -->
   {% endcache %}
   ```

3. **View-Level Caching**:
   - Cache the entire view to avoid processing the same data repeatedly.
   - Example:

   ```python
   Copy code
   from django.views.decorators.cache import cache_page

   @cache_page(60 * 15)    # Cache for 15 minutes
   def product_list(request):
   ```

```
products = Product.objects.all()
return              render(request,
'product_list.html',          {'products':
products})
```

4. **Low-Level Caching**:
   - Use Django's `cache` API for custom caching scenarios, such as storing computed data.
   - Example:

```python
Copy code
from django.core.cache import cache

result = cache.get('expensive_query')
if not result:
    result = perform_expensive_query()
    cache.set('expensive_query',    result,
timeout=300)   # Cache for 5 minutes
```

Configuring Cache Backends

1. **Using Memcached or Redis as a Cache Backend**:
   - Configure Django to use Memcached or Redis for high-performance caching.
   - Example configuration in `settings.py`:

```python
Copy code
CACHES = {
    'default': {
        'BACKEND':
'django.core.cache.backends.memcached.Mem
cachedCache',
        'LOCATION': '127.0.0.1:11211',
    }
}
```

2. **Setting Cache Timeout Values**:
   - Determine optimal cache expiration times based on data frequency and application needs.

4. Optimizing Templates for Faster Rendering

Django templates are fast, but heavy templates with nested loops or multiple database queries can slow down performance. Optimizing template rendering improves overall page load times.

Minimizing Template Complexity

1. **Avoiding Database Queries in Templates**:
   - Minimize or eliminate database queries within templates by passing all necessary data from views.
2. **Reducing Template Logic**:
   - Keep complex logic in views rather than templates, making templates lighter and faster.
3. **Using Django's Template Caching**:
   - Cache frequently used template fragments to reduce rendering time.
   - Example:

```html
Copy code
{% load cache %}
{% cache 300 product_list %}
    {% for product in products %}
        {{ product.name }}
    {% endfor %}
{% endcache %}
```

Leveraging Template Inheritance

1. **Using Template Inheritance**:
   - Create a base template with shared elements (e.g., header, footer) and extend it in other templates to avoid redundant code.
2. **Optimizing Static File Usage**:

- o Minimize CSS, JavaScript, and image files used in templates by combining and compressing files.

5. Profiling and Monitoring Performance

Profiling helps identify slow parts of an application, allowing you to target specific areas for optimization. Monitoring performance over time helps track application behavior under real-world conditions.

Profiling Tools

1. **Using Django Debug Toolbar**:
   - o Django Debug Toolbar provides insights into SQL queries, template rendering time, and more.
   - o Installation:

   ```bash
   Copy code
   pip install django-debug-toolbar
   ```

   - o **Configuration in** `settings.py`:

   ```python
   Copy code
   INSTALLED_APPS = [
       # Other apps...
       'debug_toolbar',
   ]

   MIDDLEWARE = [

   'debug_toolbar.middleware.DebugToolbarMid
   dleware',
       # Other middleware...
   ]
   ```

2. **Using Silk for Detailed Profiling**:

o Silk provides a detailed look at SQL queries, response times, and profiling information for views and middleware.
o Installation:

```bash
Copy code
pip install django-silk
```

o Configuration:

```python
Copy code
INSTALLED_APPS = [
    'silk',
    # Other apps...
]

MIDDLEWARE = [
    'silk.middleware.SilkyMiddleware',
    # Other middleware...
]
```

Monitoring in Production

1. **Using Application Monitoring Tools (e.g., New Relic):**
   o Tools like New Relic monitor performance in production, track error rates, and provide detailed insights into slow requests or high resource usage.
2. **Setting Up Logging for Performance Metrics**:
   o Log request times, database query counts, and other key metrics for monitoring performance trends.

6. Real-World Example: Applying Caching to a High-Traffic Page

Let's use caching to optimize a high-traffic blog homepage, reducing database load and improving response times.

Step 1: Implement View-Level Caching

1. **Add View-Level Caching to the Homepage**:
   - Use `cache_page` to cache the homepage view for 10 minutes, reducing load on the database for frequent requests.
   - Example:

```python
Copy code
from django.views.decorators.cache import cache_page

@cache_page(60 * 10)    # Cache for 10 minutes
def blog_homepage(request):
    posts = Post.objects.all()
    return render(request, 'blog_homepage.html', {'posts': posts})
```

Step 2: Use Template Fragment Caching

1. **Cache the Most Expensive Template Section**:
   - Cache the list of blog posts in the homepage template, allowing other parts of the page to load faster.
   - Example in `blog_homepage.html`:

```html
Copy code
{% load cache %}
{% cache 600 blog_posts %}
    <div class="posts">
        {% for post in posts %}
            <h2>{{ post.title }}</h2>
        {% endfor %}
```

```
</div>
{% endcache %}
```

Step 3: Cache Popular Database Queries

1. **Cache the Top Blog Posts Query**:
   o Cache results of commonly requested queries, such as top posts, to reduce repeated database access.
   o Example:

```python
Copy code
from django.core.cache import cache

def get_top_posts():
    top_posts = cache.get('top_posts')
    if not top_posts:
        top_posts                       =
Post.objects.order_by('-views')[:5]
        cache.set('top_posts',  top_posts,
timeout=600)
        return top_posts
```

Step 4: Use Debug Toolbar to Analyze Performance

1. **Enable Debug Toolbar for Local Testing**:
   o Use Django Debug Toolbar to view the effects of caching and check for any uncached database queries or slow template rendering.

7. Summary

In this chapter, we explored several techniques for optimizing Django application performance, including database query optimization, caching strategies, and template improvements. We provided practical examples of implementing view and template caching to improve the performance of a high-traffic page. By applying these techniques, you can reduce server load, improve user experience, and scale your Django application to handle larger workloads and higher traffic.

CHAPTER 17: DEPLOYING DJANGO APPLICATIONS TO THE WEB

Deploying a Django application involves preparing your project for production, selecting a hosting platform, and configuring the necessary tools and services for your application to run securely and efficiently. In this chapter, we'll explore best practices for preparing a Django project for deployment, examine popular hosting options, and walk through the deployment process to a cloud platform.

1. Preparing a Django Application for Production

Before deploying a Django application, it's essential to configure settings and security features that are specific to production environments.

Key Production Settings

1. **Setting `DEBUG = False`:**
   - Set `DEBUG = False` in `settings.py` to prevent sensitive error details from being displayed to users.
   - Example:

     ```python
     Copy code
     DEBUG = False
     ```

2. **Configuring `ALLOWED_HOSTS`:**

- o Set `ALLOWED_HOSTS` to the domain or IP address of your server to prevent HTTP host header attacks.
- o Example:

```python
Copy code
ALLOWED_HOSTS    =    ['yourdomain.com',
'www.yourdomain.com']
```

3. **Setting Up Static and Media Files for Production**:
   - o Configure `STATIC_ROOT` and `MEDIA_ROOT` to handle static and media files.
   - o Example:

```python
Copy code
STATIC_URL = '/static/'
STATIC_ROOT = BASE_DIR / 'staticfiles'
MEDIA_URL = '/media/'
MEDIA_ROOT = BASE_DIR / 'mediafiles'
```

4. **Using Environment Variables for Sensitive Information**:
   - o Store sensitive information such as `SECRET_KEY` in environment variables to keep them secure.
   - o Example:

```python
Copy code
import os

SECRET_KEY                              =
os.getenv('DJANGO_SECRET_KEY')
```

5. **Setting Up Security Features**:
   - o Enable security settings like `SECURE_SSL_REDIRECT`, `CSRF_COOKIE_SECURE`, and `SESSION_COOKIE_SECURE` to enforce HTTPS and secure cookies.
   - o Example:

```python
Copy code
SECURE_SSL_REDIRECT = True
CSRF_COOKIE_SECURE = True
SESSION_COOKIE_SECURE = True
```

2. Choosing a Deployment Option

There are several options for deploying Django applications, each with unique advantages and configurations. Here are some popular choices.

Common Deployment Platforms

1. **Platform-as-a-Service (PaaS)**:
    o Platforms like Heroku and PythonAnywhere handle infrastructure management, simplifying deployment for developers.
    o Examples: **Heroku, PythonAnywhere**
2. **Virtual Private Server (VPS)**:
    o VPS providers offer more control over server settings, allowing you to install software and customize configurations.
    o Examples: **DigitalOcean, Linode**
3. **Cloud Providers**:
    o Cloud providers like AWS and Google Cloud offer flexible and scalable infrastructure, making them suitable for larger applications.
    o Examples: **Amazon Web Services (AWS), Google Cloud Platform (GCP)**
4. **Container Platforms**:
    o Platforms like Docker allow you to package your application and its dependencies into containers for consistent deployment across environments.
    o Examples: **Docker, Kubernetes**

3. Deploying to Heroku

Heroku is a popular PaaS platform that simplifies the deployment process, especially for smaller projects or prototypes. Let's go through the steps to deploy a Django app on Heroku.

Step 1: Prepare the Project for Heroku

1. **Install Gunicorn**:
   - Gunicorn is a WSGI HTTP server required for running Django applications in production on Heroku.
   - Example:

   ```bash
   Copy code
   pip install gunicorn
   ```

2. **Create a `Procfile`**:
   - Heroku uses a `Procfile` to know how to start your application. Create a file named `Procfile` in the root directory with the following content:

   ```bash
   Copy code
   web: gunicorn yourproject.wsgi --log-file -
   ```

3. **Install `django-heroku`**:
   - The `django-heroku` package automatically configures your Django settings for Heroku.
   - Example:

   ```bash
   Copy code
   pip install django-heroku
   ```

4. **Update `settings.py`:**
   - Import `django_heroku` and apply Heroku-specific settings at the bottom of `settings.py`.
   - Example:

   ```python
   Copy code
   import django_heroku
   django_heroku.settings(locals())
   ```

Step 2: Set Up the Database for Production

1. **Configure PostgreSQL:**
   - Heroku uses PostgreSQL as the default database for Django applications. Use `dj-database-url` to handle database configurations.
   - Installation:

   ```bash
   Copy code
   pip install dj-database-url
   ```

   - Update `settings.py` to configure the database.

   ```python
   Copy code
   import dj_database_url
   DATABASES = {
       'default':
   dj_database_url.config(conn_max_age=600)
   }
   ```

Step 3: Deploy to Heroku

1. **Create a Git Repository:**
   - If you haven't already, initialize a Git repository:

   ```bash
   ```

```
Copy code
git init
git add .
git commit -m "Initial commit"
```

2. **Create a Heroku App**:
   o Log into Heroku and create a new application:

```bash
Copy code
heroku login
heroku create your-app-name
```

3. **Push to Heroku**:
   o Deploy your application by pushing the code to Heroku:

```bash
Copy code
git push heroku main
```

4. **Run Migrations and Collect Static Files**:
   o After deployment, run database migrations and collect static files:

```bash
Copy code
heroku run python manage.py migrate
heroku run python manage.py collectstatic
--noinput
```

4. Deploying to DigitalOcean

DigitalOcean is a VPS provider that offers more control over server configurations. This section provides a general outline for deploying a Django app on DigitalOcean using Ubuntu and Gunicorn with Nginx.

Step 1: Set Up a Droplet (Virtual Server)

1. **Create a Droplet**:
   - Log into DigitalOcean, create a new Droplet, and select Ubuntu as the operating system.
2. **Connect to the Droplet**:
   - Use SSH to connect to your server:

   ```bash
   Copy code
   ssh root@your_droplet_ip
   ```

Step 2: Install Required Software

1. **Update the Package List**:
   - Update the list of available packages:

   ```bash
   Copy code
   sudo apt update
   ```

2. **Install Python, Pip, and Virtualenv**:
   - Install Python, Pip, and Virtualenv:

   ```bash
   Copy code
   sudo apt install python3 python3-pip python3-venv
   ```

3. **Install and Set Up PostgreSQL**:
   - Install PostgreSQL and create a new user and database for your Django app.
   - Example commands:

   ```bash
   Copy code
   sudo apt install postgresql postgresql-contrib
   sudo -u postgres createuser --interactive
   ```

```
sudo -u postgres createdb yourdbname
```

Step 3: Configure the Django Application

1. **Clone the Django Project**:
   - Clone your Django project from GitHub or upload it directly.
2. **Create a Virtual Environment and Install Requirements**:
   - Create a virtual environment and install dependencies:

   ```bash
   Copy code
   python3 -m venv venv
   source venv/bin/activate
   pip install -r requirements.txt
   ```

3. **Set Up Gunicorn**:
   - Install Gunicorn and configure it as the application server for your project.
   - Example:

   ```bash
   Copy code
   pip install gunicorn
   gunicorn            --workers        3
   yourproject.wsgi:application
   ```

Step 4: Set Up Nginx as a Reverse Proxy

1. **Install Nginx**:
   - Install Nginx to serve as a reverse proxy.
   - Example:

   ```bash
   Copy code
   sudo apt install nginx
   ```

2. **Configure Nginx for Django**:

- o Set up a new Nginx configuration file for your Django project.
- o Example configuration:

```nginx
nginx
Copy code
server {
    listen 80;
    server_name your_domain_or_ip;

    location / {
        proxy_pass http://127.0.0.1:8000;
        proxy_set_header Host $host;
        proxy_set_header          X-Real-IP
$remote_addr;
        proxy_set_header    X-Forwarded-For
$proxy_add_x_forwarded_for;
        proxy_set_header X-Forwarded-Proto
$scheme;
    }

    location /static/ {
        alias /path/to/your/static/files;
    }

    location /media/ {
        alias /path/to/your/media/files;
    }
}
```

3. **Restart Nginx**:
   - o Restart Nginx to apply the new configuration:

```bash
bash
Copy code
sudo systemctl restart nginx
```

5. Deploying Static and Media Files

Handling static and media files in production is essential for serving assets efficiently.

Using a Content Delivery Network (CDN)

1. **Why Use a CDN**:
   - A CDN helps deliver static and media files faster by serving them from servers closer to users.
2. **Setting Up a CDN**:
   - Services like AWS S3, Cloudflare, or DigitalOcean Spaces can serve static and media files. Update STATIC_URL and MEDIA_URL to use the CDN URL.

Collecting Static Files in Production

1. **Run collectstatic to Gather Static Files**:
   - Use the collectstatic command to collect all static files in the STATIC_ROOT directory.
   - Example:

```bash
Copy code
python manage.py collectstatic
```

6. Testing and Monitoring Your Deployment

Once deployed, monitor the application for errors, performance issues, and security vulnerabilities.

Using Application Monitoring Tools

1. **Install Monitoring Tools**:
   - Tools like New Relic, Datadog, and Sentry can monitor performance, errors, and logs.
2. **Set Up Alerts for Critical Events**:

- o Configure alerts to notify you of errors, server downtime, or unusual spikes in resource usage.

Conducting a Post-Deployment Test

1. **Test Key Features**:
   - o Test core features of your application to ensure everything works as expected in the production environment.
2. **Check for Security and Performance Issues**:
   - o Review security settings and use tools like PageSpeed Insights to check for performance optimization opportunities.

7. Summary

In this chapter, we covered essential steps for deploying a Django application, including preparing for production, selecting a hosting platform, and configuring the server and application for deployment. We walked through the deployment process on popular platforms like Heroku and DigitalOcean and discussed best practices for handling static and media files in production. By following these steps, you can successfully deploy and maintain a Django application in a production environment, providing a seamless experience for end users.

CHAPTER 18: SECURING YOUR DJANGO APPLICATION

Security is paramount in web development, as vulnerabilities can lead to data breaches, loss of user trust, and potential legal issues. Django offers built-in tools to mitigate common security risks, and understanding these features is essential for building secure applications. In this chapter, we'll explore Django's security mechanisms, best practices for secure coding, and provide a practical example of securing user authentication and protecting sensitive data.

1. Overview of Web Application Security

Web application security involves implementing measures to protect data, prevent unauthorized access, and guard against malicious attacks. Understanding potential threats and how to counteract them is key to maintaining a secure Django application.

Common Web Security Vulnerabilities

1. **Cross-Site Scripting (XSS):**
    - Attackers inject malicious scripts into a trusted website, which are then executed in users' browsers.
2. **Cross-Site Request Forgery (CSRF):**
    - Attackers trick users into performing unwanted actions on a website, exploiting the user's authenticated session.

3. **SQL Injection**:
   - Malicious SQL code is injected into queries, allowing attackers to access or manipulate the database.
4. **Insecure Direct Object References (IDOR)**:
   - Attackers access data by manipulating identifiers (e.g., user IDs) in URLs or forms without proper authorization checks.
5. **Sensitive Data Exposure**:
   - Improper handling of sensitive data (e.g., passwords, payment details) can lead to data breaches.

2. Django's Built-In Security Features

Django provides several security features by default, helping to prevent common vulnerabilities without extensive manual configuration.

CSRF Protection

1. **CSRF Tokens**:
   - Django automatically protects against CSRF by including tokens in forms, ensuring requests are genuine.
   - Example:

```html
Copy code
<form method="post">
    {% csrf_token %}
    <!-- form fields -->
    <button type="submit">Submit</button>
</form>
```

2. **Adding CSRF Tokens to AJAX Requests**:

o For AJAX requests, manually add the CSRF token to headers.
o Example:

```javascript
Copy code
$.ajaxSetup({
    headers:    {    "X-CSRFToken":    "{{
csrf_token }}" }
});
```

XSS Protection

1. **Auto-Escaping in Templates**:
   o Django escapes output by default, preventing XSS attacks by not allowing JavaScript or HTML code to execute.
   o Example:

```html
Copy code
{{ user_input }}   <!-- Auto-escaped by
Django -->
```

2. **Using `safe` Carefully**:
   o Use |safe with caution, as it marks content as safe to render, bypassing Django's escaping mechanism.

SQL Injection Protection

1. **Using ORM Queries**:
   o Django's ORM automatically parameterizes queries, preventing SQL injection.
   o Example:

```python
Copy code
```

```
user = User.objects.get(username=username)
# ORM handles query safely
```

2. **Avoiding Raw SQL Queries**:
   - o Avoid using raw SQL unless absolutely necessary, and if used, always sanitize inputs.

3. Securing User Authentication and Sessions

User authentication and session management are essential parts of web application security, as they manage how users are identified and authorized.

Securing Passwords

1. **Using Django's Password Hashing**:
   - o Django hashes and salts passwords automatically, using PBKDF2 by default.
   - o Example of creating a user:

```python
Copy code
user                                    =
User.objects.create_user(username='john',
password='mypassword')
```

2. **Setting Password Policies**:
   - o Enforce strong password requirements by customizing password validators in settings.py.
   - o Example:

```python
Copy code
AUTH_PASSWORD_VALIDATORS = [
```

214

```
        {
            'NAME':
'django.contrib.auth.password_validation.
UserAttributeSimilarityValidator',
        },
        {
            'NAME':
'django.contrib.auth.password_validation.
MinimumLengthValidator',
            'OPTIONS': {'min_length': 8},
        },
    ]
```

Session Security

1. **Using Secure Cookies**:
   - Enable `SESSION_COOKIE_SECURE` and `CSRF_COOKIE_SECURE` to ensure cookies are only sent over HTTPS.
   - Example:

   ```python
   Copy code
   SESSION_COOKIE_SECURE = True
   CSRF_COOKIE_SECURE = True
   ```

2. **Implementing Session Timeout**:
   - Set `SESSION_COOKIE_AGE` to control the duration of user sessions.
   - Example:

   ```python
   Copy code
   SESSION_COOKIE_AGE = 1800   # 30 minutes
   ```

4. Enforcing HTTPS and Secure Headers

HTTPS encrypts data between the client and server, preventing data interception. Additional security headers protect against certain types of attacks.

Enforcing HTTPS

1. **Redirecting HTTP to HTTPS**:
   o Set `SECURE_SSL_REDIRECT` to force HTTPS.
   o Example:

   ```python
   Copy code
   SECURE_SSL_REDIRECT = True
   ```

2. **Using HSTS (HTTP Strict Transport Security)**:
   o Enable `SECURE_HSTS_SECONDS` to instruct browsers to only access the site via HTTPS.
   o Example:

   ```python
   Copy code
   SECURE_HSTS_SECONDS = 31536000   # One year
   ```

Adding Security Headers

1. **Content Security Policy (CSP)**:
   o Add a CSP header to limit sources for scripts, styles, and other resources.
   o Example:

   ```python
   Copy code
   from django.middleware.security import SecurityMiddleware
   response['Content-Security-Policy'] = "default-src 'self'"
   ```

2. **X-Content-Type-Options**:
   o Add the `X-Content-Type-Options` header to prevent browsers from interpreting files as a different MIME type.
   o Example:

```python
Copy code
response['X-Content-Type-Options'] = 'nosniff'
```

5. Best Practices for Secure Django Development

Beyond built-in features, secure coding practices can further safeguard your application against attacks.

Protecting Sensitive Data

1. **Using Environment Variables**:
   o Store sensitive data, such as database credentials and API keys, in environment variables.
   o Example:

```python
Copy code
DATABASES = {
    'default': {
        'ENGINE':
'django.db.backends.postgresql',
        'NAME': os.getenv('DB_NAME'),
        'USER': os.getenv('DB_USER'),
        'PASSWORD':
os.getenv('DB_PASSWORD'),
        'HOST': os.getenv('DB_HOST'),
        'PORT': '5432',
    }
}
```

2. **Encrypting Sensitive Information**:
   o For highly sensitive data, use encryption libraries like `cryptography`.

Avoiding Exposed Debug Information

1. **Setting DEBUG = `False` in Production**:
   o Always set `DEBUG` = `False` to avoid exposing detailed error messages in production.
2. **Using Error Logging**:
   o Configure logging to capture errors while keeping them hidden from users.
   o Example:

```python
Copy code
LOGGING = {
    'version': 1,
    'disable_existing_loggers': False,
    'handlers': {
        'file': {
            'level': 'ERROR',
            'class':
'logging.FileHandler',
            'filename':
'/path/to/error.log',
        },
    },
    'loggers': {
        'django': {
            'handlers': ['file'],
            'level': 'ERROR',
            'propagate': True,
        },
    },
}
```

6. Real-World Example: Implementing Secure Login and Protecting Sensitive Data

Let's apply these security practices by implementing a secure login system and protecting user-sensitive data.

Step 1: Secure the User Login Process

1. **Enable HTTPS for Secure Transmission**:
   o Redirect all HTTP requests to HTTPS and set up HSTS to ensure secure data transmission.
2. **Set Secure Cookies**:
   o Configure `SESSION_COOKIE_SECURE` and `CSRF_COOKIE_SECURE` to prevent cookies from being sent over non-secure connections.
3. **Enforce Strong Passwords**:
   o Use Django's password validators to enforce a minimum length and complexity for passwords.
4. **Implement Brute-Force Protection**:
   o Consider using Django's `django-axes` package to lock out users after too many failed login attempts.
   o Example:

   ```bash
   bash
   Copy code
   pip install django-axes
   ```

Step 2: Protect Sensitive User Information

1. **Encrypting Sensitive Fields**:
   o Use `cryptography` to encrypt fields such as SSNs or credit card numbers before storing them in the database.
   o Example:

   ```python
   python
   Copy code
   from cryptography.fernet import Fernet
   ```

```
key = Fernet.generate_key()
cipher_suite = Fernet(key)
encrypted_text                          =
cipher_suite.encrypt(b"Sensitive Data")
```

2. **Restricting Access to Sensitive Views**:

o Use permissions or roles to restrict access to views displaying sensitive data.

o Example:

```python
Copy code
from django.contrib.auth.decorators import
user_passes_test

def staff_required(user):
    return user.is_staff

@user_passes_test(staff_required)
def view_sensitive_data(request):
    # Logic for sensitive data
```

3. **Audit Logging for Access to Sensitive Data**:

o Log access to sensitive data, such as who accessed it and when, to provide an audit trail.

o Example:

```python
Copy code
import logging

logger = logging.getLogger(__name__)

def view_sensitive_data(request):
    logger.info(f"User           {request.user}
accessed        sensitive        data        at
{timezone.now()}")
```

7. Summary

In this chapter, we explored Django's security features, best practices for secure coding, and techniques to protect against common vulnerabilities like XSS, CSRF, and SQL injection. We also provided a practical example of implementing secure login and safeguarding sensitive data. By following these practices, you can create a Django application that prioritizes security, protects user data, and minimizes the risk of potential attacks.

CHAPTER 19: INTEGRATING WEB SOCKETS FOR REAL-TIME FEATURES

Real-time features, like live chat, notifications, and activity updates, enhance user experience by allowing instant communication and data updates. WebSockets are a key technology for implementing these features, enabling two-way communication between the client and server. In this chapter, we'll explore how to use Django Channels to handle WebSocket connections, build real-time communication capabilities, and provide a practical example of adding live updates to a dashboard.

1. Introduction to WebSockets and Django Channels

WebSockets are a protocol that enables persistent, full-duplex communication between the client and server, allowing data to be sent in real-time. Django Channels extends Django to handle WebSocket connections and enables asynchronous communication, making it a powerful tool for building real-time applications.

Why Use WebSockets for Real-Time Applications?

1. **Instant Data Updates**:
    o   WebSockets enable instant updates, ideal for applications requiring live data, such as chat or notifications.
2. **Reduced Latency**:

- ○ Since WebSockets maintain an open connection, they reduce the overhead of repeatedly opening and closing connections, lowering latency for real-time features.

3. **Asynchronous Communication**:
   - ○ Django Channels allows for asynchronous processing, so your server can handle multiple connections simultaneously, even under heavy load.

2. Setting Up Django Channels

To start using WebSockets in Django, you need to install and configure Django Channels, which adds support for asynchronous requests, including WebSockets.

Installing Django Channels

1. **Install Django Channels**:
   - ○ Use pip to install Django Channels and an asynchronous Redis server to manage WebSocket connections.
   - ○ Example:

```bash
Copy code
pip install channels channels_redis
```

2. **Updating `settings.py` for Channels**:
   - ○ Add `channels` to `INSTALLED_APPS` and specify an ASGI (Asynchronous Server Gateway Interface) application.
   - ○ Example:

```python
Copy code
INSTALLED_APPS = [
    # Other apps...
    'channels',
]

ASGI_APPLICATION                    =
'yourproject.asgi.application'

CHANNEL_LAYERS = {
    'default': {
        'BACKEND':
'channels_redis.core.RedisChannelLayer',
        'CONFIG': {
            "hosts":          [('127.0.0.1',
6379)],
        },
    },
]
```

3. **Creating an ASGI Configuration**:
   o **Define an** asgi.py **file in your project directory,
     similar to** wsgi.py, **to handle asynchronous
     requests.**
   o **Example** (yourproject/asgi.py):

```python
Copy code
import os
from        django.core.asgi        import
get_asgi_application
from        channels.routing        import
ProtocolTypeRouter, URLRouter
from         channels.auth           import
AuthMiddlewareStack
import yourapp.routing

os.environ.setdefault('DJANGO_SETTINGS_MO
DULE', 'yourproject.settings')

application = ProtocolTypeRouter({
    "http": get_asgi_application(),
    "websocket": AuthMiddlewareStack(
```

```
URLRouter(

yourapp.routing.websocket_urlpatterns
        )
    ),
})
```

3. Setting Up WebSocket Routing

WebSocket routing defines how WebSocket connections are handled, similar to how URL routing works for HTTP requests. Channels uses routing.py to configure WebSocket endpoints.

Defining WebSocket Routes

1. **Create a routing.py File in Your App**:
   - o This file defines URL patterns for WebSocket connections.
   - o **Example** (yourapp/routing.py):

   ```python
   python
   Copy code
   from django.urls import re_path
   from . import consumers

   websocket_urlpatterns = [

   re_path(r'ws/chat/(?P<room_name>\w+)/$',
   consumers.ChatConsumer.as_asgi()),
   ]
   ```

2. **Register WebSocket Routes in asgi.py**:
   - o Import websocket_urlpatterns from your app and register them under the websocket protocol in asgi.py.

4. Creating Consumers for Real-Time Communication

Consumers are similar to Django views but handle WebSocket requests. They define the behavior for handling incoming messages, connecting, and disconnecting WebSocket clients.

Building a Basic WebSocket Consumer

1. **Create a WebSocket Consumer**:
   o Define a consumer that manages WebSocket connections, sending and receiving messages.
   o Example:

```python
Copy code
from channels.generic.websocket import
AsyncWebsocketConsumer
import json

class
ChatConsumer(AsyncWebsocketConsumer):
    async def connect(self):
        self.room_name                =
self.scope['url_route']['kwargs']['room_n
ame']
        self.room_group_name          =
f'chat_{self.room_name}'

        # Join room group
        await
self.channel_layer.group_add(
            self.room_group_name,
            self.channel_name
        )

        await self.accept()

    async     def     disconnect(self,
close_code):
        # Leave room group
```

```
        await
self.channel_layer.group_discard(
        self.room_group_name,
        self.channel_name
    )

    async def receive(self, text_data):
        text_data_json                =
json.loads(text_data)
        message                       =
text_data_json['message']

        # Send message to room group
        await
self.channel_layer.group_send(
        self.room_group_name,
        {
            'type': 'chat_message',
            'message': message
        }
    )

    async def chat_message(self, event):
        message = event['message']

        # Send message to WebSocket
        await
self.send(text_data=json.dumps({
        'message': message
    }))
```

2. **Handling WebSocket Events**:
   o Define functions like connect, disconnect, and receive to handle each stage of a WebSocket connection, including sending and receiving messages.

5. Setting Up Frontend JavaScript for WebSocket Connections

For real-time features to work, the frontend must establish a WebSocket connection and handle incoming messages.

Creating a WebSocket Connection in JavaScript

1. **Establish a WebSocket Connection**:
   o Use JavaScript to open a WebSocket connection to the server and handle events.
   o Example:

```javascript
javascript
Copy code
const roomName = "{{ room_name }}";
const chatSocket = new WebSocket(
    'ws://'   +   window.location.host   +
'/ws/chat/' + roomName + '/'
);

chatSocket.onmessage = function(e) {
    const data = JSON.parse(e.data);
    document.querySelector('#chat-
log').value += (data.message + '\n');
};

chatSocket.onclose = function(e) {
    console.error('Chat    socket    closed
unexpectedly');
};

document.querySelector('#chat-message-
input').focus();
document.querySelector('#chat-message-
input').onkeyup = function(e) {
    if (e.keyCode === 13) {  // Enter key
        const              message              =
document.querySelector('#chat-message-
input').value;

chatSocket.send(JSON.stringify({'message'
: message}));
        document.querySelector('#chat-
message-input').value = '';
    }
};
```

2. **Sending Messages**:
   - o Use `send` to send JSON-formatted messages to the WebSocket server.
3. **Handling Received Messages**:
   - o Use the `onmessage` event to listen for incoming data and update the DOM in real-time.

6. Real-World Example: Building a Live Chat Feature

Let's apply these concepts by building a live chat feature where users can join chat rooms and communicate in real-time.

Step 1: Define the Chat Room Model (Optional)

1. **Create a Simple Room Model**:
   - o You can create a model to manage rooms if needed.
   - o Example:

```python
Copy code
from django.db import models

class Room(models.Model):
    name                        =
models.CharField(max_length=100,
unique=True)
```

Step 2: Create the Chat Consumer

1. **Define a Chat Consumer for Real-Time Messaging**:
   - o Implement a consumer as shown earlier to manage WebSocket connections and broadcast messages to all users in a room.

Step 3: Set Up WebSocket Routing

1. **Define the Chat WebSocket Route**:
   - Use `re_path` to define the WebSocket route for chat rooms.
   - Example:

   ```python
   python
   Copy code
   websocket_urlpatterns = [

   re_path(r'ws/chat/(?P<room_name>\w+)/$',
   consumers.ChatConsumer.as_asgi()),
   ]
   ```

Step 4: Create Frontend for Real-Time Chat

1. **Set Up HTML and JavaScript**:
   - Add an HTML template with JavaScript to connect to the WebSocket and display messages.
   - Example (`chat_room.html`):

   ```html
   html
   Copy code
   <div>
       <textarea    id="chat-log"    cols="100"
   rows="20" readonly></textarea><br>
       <input            id="chat-message-input"
   type="text" size="100"><br>
   </div>

   <script    src="{%    static    'js/chat.js'
   %}"></script>
   ```

2. **Implement JavaScript to Handle WebSocket Connections**:
   - Use JavaScript to handle the WebSocket connection, send messages, and display incoming messages.

7. Securing WebSocket Connections

Real-time applications should implement authentication and permissions to control access.

Adding Authentication to WebSocket Connections

1. **Using `AuthMiddlewareStack`:**
   o Django Channels provides `AuthMiddlewareStack` to manage user sessions and authenticate WebSocket connections.
   o **Example in** `asgi.py`:

```python
Copy code
from channels.auth import AuthMiddlewareStack

application = ProtocolTypeRouter({
    "websocket": AuthMiddlewareStack(
        URLRouter(
            yourapp.routing.websocket_urlpatterns
        )
    ),
})
```

2. **Restricting Access to Chat Rooms:**
   o Use Django permissions or custom checks in the consumer to limit access to authorized users only.

8. Testing and Debugging WebSocket Connections

Testing WebSocket connections requires different approaches from standard HTTP testing due to their persistent nature.

Testing Consumers

1. **Using Channels Test Framework**:
   - o Django Channels provides tools for testing consumers and simulating WebSocket connections.
   - o Example:

```python
Copy code
from        channels.testing        import
WebsocketCommunicator
import pytest
from yourproject.asgi import application

@pytest.mark.asyncio
async def test_chat_consumer():
    communicator                         =
WebsocketCommunicator(application,
"/ws/chat/test/")
    connected,    subprotocol    =    await
communicator.connect()
    assert connected
    await
communicator.send_json_to({"message":
"hello"})
    response            =            await
communicator.receive_json_from()
    assert response["message"] == "hello"
    await communicator.disconnect()
```

2. **Debugging WebSocket Connections**:
   - o Use Django Channels logs and WebSocket status codes to troubleshoot issues, such as unexpected disconnections.

9. Summary

In this chapter, we explored how to integrate WebSockets in Django using Django Channels, covering the setup, WebSocket routing, and consumer creation. We also demonstrated how to create a live chat feature with real-time communication between users. By leveraging

Django Channels, you can build engaging real-time features such as chat systems, notifications, and live dashboards, enhancing the interactivity and responsiveness of your Django application.

www.ingramcontent.com/pod-product-compliance
Lightning Source LLC
La Vergne TN
LVHW051322050326
832903LV00031B/3307